SUSIE ASEKA BROOKS

HE REALLY IS MY FATHER

Pleasant Word
A Division of WINEPRESS PUBLISHING

© 2006 by Susie A. Brooks. All rights reserved.

Pleasant Word (a division of WinePress Publishing, PO Box 428, Enumclaw, WA 98022) functions only as book publisher. As such, the ultimate design, content, editorial accuracy, and views expressed or implied in this work are those of the author.

No part of this publication may be reproduced, stored in a retrieval system or transmitted in any way by any means—electronic, mechanical, photocopy, recording or otherwise—without the prior permission of the copyright holder, except as provided by USA copyright law.

Unless otherwise noted, all Scriptures are taken from the Holy Bible, New International Version, Copyright © 1973, 1978, 1984 by the International Bible Society. Used by permission of Zondervan Publishing House. The "NIV" and "New International Version" trademarks are registered in the United States Patent and Trademark Office by International Bible Society.

Scripture references marked KJV are taken from the King James Version of the Bible.

Scripture references marked NASB are taken from the New American Standard Bible, © 1960, 1963, 1968, 1971, 1972, 1973, 1975, 1977 by The Lockman Foundation. Used by permission.

ISBN 1-4141-0491-X
Library of Congress Catalog Card Number: 2006904286

Thuis bij de hemelse Vader

Willem Johannes Bouw

February 20, 1940 – September 5, 2003

Dedication

To my son,
Seraiah Jonathan Brooks
May you always know that God really is your Father

Table of Contents

Acknowledgements   XI

1. Aboard KLM Flight 6042   13
2. My Childhood   27
3. The End of My Childhood   53
4. Dividing the Five   63
5. Shock to the System   71
6. Margy and I   83
7. Enduring   89
8. My Conversion   105
9. Coup d'Etat   111
10. The Teen Challenge   119
11. Plateau   131
12. I Fly Away   143
13. Becoming a Daughter   149

14. Groningen	159
15. Prince Charming	167
16. He Really Is My Father	177
About the Author	189

Acknowledgements

Soon after Daddy's passing in September, 2003, I felt a strong desire to write a book in honor of his life. For fifteen years, he had offered me love and hope like only a father can give. As the writing developed, it suddenly became clear that God had used this relationship with Daddy to reveal Himself as my true heavenly Father.

Heartfelt gratitude goes to Suzanne Ray for hours spent reading my manuscript twice and offering honest feedback and guidance, which helped me become a better writer.

I would like to also thank my husband, who patiently read all the pages out loud and offered helpful suggestions, even though he knew the story.

Noel Piper, Lucille Travis, Lois Swenson, Ruth Knutson, Marla Nelson, Njeri Mbugua and others whose names I have not mentioned: thank you for all your help and support during this time. You are great editors!

Chapter 1

Aboard KLM Flight 6042

"Flight attendants prepare for departure," the captain's voice crackled over the loud speakers into the crowded Boeing 747 as passengers scrambled to find room for carry-on luggage.

From the corner of my teary eye I could see blurred images dressed in sky blue hurrying down the aisles making sure seatbelts were fastened and seats were positioned upright before take off. Occasionally one would stop to make sure the baggage compartments were secured.

"Would you like me to move over so you can have this spare seat?" the Indian gentleman seated on my right asked, and he started moving before I could answer. I hadn't been assigned a window seat, but under the circumstances I would have been happy with even a floor space, as long as my five-and-a-half month-old son was content. It was my first trip to Holland in five years. The last time I'd flown from Minneapolis to Amsterdam had been after completing my exchange program and internship in America (part of my degree requirement) to graduate from the renowned International Business School.

"Thank you," I managed to say, readjusting my seatbelt and picking up the diaper bag to place it on the now empty seat to my right. A spare seat was certainly welcome, but I desperately hoped my new Indian friend wouldn't engage me in conversation with countless questions, ranging from the number of children I had to whether people in my country speak English.

Across from us sat an Indian woman dressed in a beautiful lavender sari, and next to her was an older Indian man, probably her father. Having grown up in Kenya where Indians dominated the retail industry, I was very familiar with their outward appearance and way of speaking. The women held onto their cultural style of dress, which as a little girl I had always admired. Indians made their first appearance in East Africa in the late 1800s, when the British colonialists brought them to work on the East African railway line. Even though their original presence was associated with the building of the railway, after Kenya's independence they had remained in the country. They took over the British-owned businesses, a role that assigned them a status slightly below the white expatriates, yet above the black locals, forcing us to view them as our superiors. Even now as

I accepted the kindness of the Indian gentleman, it was still an honor to be acknowledged by a person from a race that had rarely socialized with my kind during my childhood.

The woman in the sari turned her head to the gentleman sitting in my row and engaged him in a conversation—or was it an argument? The rapid, high-pitched tone of Indian languages had always sounded like anger to me. Noticing a gentle smile on the man's face, I was relieved to see it was a friendly conversation. Slowly beginning to relax in my seat, I contemplated whether God, understanding the burden I was carrying, had gone ahead of me and placed just the right person next to me.

Should I tell this man how sad I feel? I wondered gently shifting my sleeping son from my left arm to my right. I've been known to wear my heart on my sleeve, and at that moment I could easily have stood up and told everyone on that flight just why I was traveling alone with my infant, making this urgent three-day trip to Holland. Instead, I settled for a simple introduction.

"I'm Susie and this is my son, Seraiah."

"Nice to meet you! You have a beautiful baby." My heart warmed up immediately, just like every mother's does when her child is praised.

"I'm Raju and that is my wife," he continued, pointing to the Indian woman by the window. "Are you from the Twin Cities?"

"Yes, but I am originally from Kenya," I answered nonchalantly, unable to enjoy any conversation unrelated to the purpose of my trip. In the next few minutes Raju told me that he worked at the University of Minnesota as an advanced genetic analyst at the biomedical genomics center and he and his wife were on their way to Amsterdam for a six-week vacation.

Vacation, I thought. How I wished my trip was a vacation. It wasn't. While I'd cried with heaviness of heart on previous plane trips, this sadness was different. It was a sorrow I had known I would one day experience, but I had dreaded the day the phone call came. Nothing ever prepares you for such a reality—my beloved father was dead.

The phone call had come on Saturday, September 6, at 2:00 p.m. My husband Steve and I had just sat down to a late lunch of brats and corn on the cob. I'd just returned from a faculty development morning at Bethel University, where I was in the first year of my teaching career. I have never experienced a premonition, but that day at the morning session I'd found myself wondering what I would do in the event that I received a phone call telling me something bad had happened. I remember looking around the room, first at the faculty moderator, then at the others in the room. Would the moderator come to me and put his arms around me and comfort me? Would everyone surround me, pray for me, and bring me Kleenex so I could wipe my tears and blow my nose? Would my supervisor, who was at the same event, drive me home or ask someone else to because I would be too sad and too emotional to drive?

I had quickly snapped out of that unusual train of thought and tried to concentrate on what was being said. I was supposed to have been an adjunct instructor in the Business Management program, but the course assigned to me had not filled up enough to be profitable. The year before, I had successfully designed a different course and had received great reviews from the first group of students. But somehow I still wanted approval from this group of men and women, who possessed the very essence of what I wanted to be: a recognized, respected, admired university professor. Why did I feel such a high need for recognition in my professional life? Why did it hurt so much when no one mentioned the small role I played in the development of the soon-to-be-launched doctoral program? Was my earlier diversion one of those self-deprecating scenarios that often ran through my mind?

Since beginning work at Bethel, I had occasionally found myself plagued by a strong sense of inadequacy. I enjoyed the occasional encouragement from my supervisor, but when surrounded by the various Ph.D. holders,

I often shied away from participating in discussions for fear of making a fool of myself. Daddy had always told everyone how smart I was. Sometimes I thought he exaggerated just so I could live up to his belief in me. Even though I was intending to begin work on my doctorate, I had little confidence in my academic accomplishments. Daddy's constant affirmation had succeeded in minimizing the self-talk regarding my inadequacy, caused by years of hearing that I did not amount to anything. Before Daddy, I had not even been considered college material. My whole sense of worth had been so deeply tied to what others thought of me.

As I sat at the same table with these academic giants, having earned my way into this unique world of higher education, I still felt inferior, almost as if I needed permission to be part of the clique. A small, still voice from deep down whispered condemning words, telling me I didn't belong. Why couldn't I fully believe what Daddy had told me? When he took me in, he helped me realize for the first time that perhaps I was somebody, that I could become anything I wanted to be. Why did I need to hear over and over again that I was just like anybody else? Would I ever change the disparaging tape that continuously played in my head?

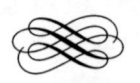

When the phone had rung, Steve was sitting at the kitchen table next to me. He rose to pick up the handheld receiver from the kitchen counter.

"Hello…Yes, this is Mr. Brooks…How are you Gisbert?…"

Gisbert? Why would my brother Gisbert be calling? Daddy always calls. Is Daddy okay? All these thoughts rushed though my mind as Steve handed me the phone. I quickly shifted my son onto my left arm, pushed my plate aside, and took the phone.

"Hi, Gisbert, how are you?…No, I didn't hear…Oh no, what happened? …Uh-huh…No, I didn't hear anything…We didn't receive any of the emails…How is he doing now?…Nooooo! Nooooo! Daddy can't be gone!"

My voice broke into uncontrollable crying. Gisbert, on the other side of the line, started crying too. Steve, sensing what was happening, walked toward me with tears running down his face. He placed his arms around me, and we cried for what seemed like several minutes. A sniffling sound through the receiver reminded me that Gisbert was still on the phone.

"Gisbert, I'm so sorry. When did this happen?… Yesterday around 4:00 p.m.?…This is so sudden…I am so sorry…"

We continued to talk for a while. By this time I was lying on the floor. Since everyone was so overcome with emotion, we agreed that I would call later to find out details about the funeral.

***

Daddy can't be dead, I thought aloud as I turned around to face Steve. He had joined me on the floor, where I was lying in a fetal position. My eyes shifted to look at the phone, still in my hand. I stared at it accusingly, as if it, in itself, was the object guilty of the terrible news. I handed it to Steve, not wanting anything more to do with it.

"Where is Seraiah?" I asked in alarm. I didn't remember what I'd done with him.

"He's okay," Steve responded gently.

As my maternal instinct took over, I rushed across the room to head for the stairs toward my son's bedroom. Just then I noticed him lying peacefully in his infant portable car seat in the middle of the kitchen floor, almost as though he had just miraculously appeared. Relieved, I moved toward Steve and collapsed in his arms and began to sob.

I cried for several minutes, while Steve gently rocked me back and forth, consoling me as I had so often consoled little Seraiah. I thought of him and wondered if he would understand or even notice what was happening. I hated being in this state—I was supposed to be the strong one in his world. I slowly withdrew from his hold and moved over to where Seraiah was still resting peacefully. His eyes were open, preoccupied by a toy hanging from the seat handle above him. Sensing my presence he looked at me and smiled, oblivious of my state of mind. At that moment, as I looked into his trusting eyes, I determined to be as courageous as I could. He was young and needed me to be brave. I picked him up from the seat, kissed his forehead, and held him close to my chest. Steve moved closer to join us. He placed his arms around the two of us. Being the pastor that he was, he started to pray, asking God to give us strength during this time of grief. He prayed that the Lord would guide our steps as we set in motion plans to attend the funeral to be held in Utrecht.

Utrecht, Netherlands. My mind wandered off as Steve continued to pray. *Why had I chosen to live so far away from Daddy?* I had not seen him since my wedding two years earlier. No one else from my family had been able to attend the wedding, since the attack on the World Trade Center earlier that month had resulted in flight cancellations and tighter measures on the issuance of visas to the United States. Both Daddy and Mommy, who did not need visas, had chosen to come despite the protests from their other children. They had arrived on Monday before the wedding and spent their time enjoying the sunny weather that had surprised Minnesotans by remaining in the mid 70s. It was early fall and the colors of the leaves on the trees had peaked, displaying shades of orange, red, and yellow. Daddy was so impressed with the beauty of the Minnesota fall that he spent most of that week outdoors. He loved to lie in the sun. It had been fun to watch him, completely lost in this rare Minnesota warmth, taking a deserved break from the demands of his life of ministry.

"Amen," Steve said as he concluded his prayer, startling me from my thoughts. "What would you like us to do next?" he asked.

I needed to make some phone calls. One friend I needed to contact was Nancy Brydges. We had known Nancy and her husband Bob for close to four years. They were involved with a Christian organization that sent them to Kenya every two years, and since that was my native country, our friendship had developed naturally because of our common interest in Kenya's affairs. Once in a while, when they returned from their trips to Kenya, they would bring us items not readily available in America. In addition to our mutual interest in Kenya, Nancy was proud that she had introduced Steve and me to each other. Because of these connections, she was a friend I always called whenever there was any major event in our lives.

"Hello, this is the Brydges!" I heard the familiar voice that came as a temporary comfort to my troubled heart. I wanted to blurt out the news of Daddy's death as if telling it would ease the deep sadness I felt. But having been constantly reminded to guard my emotions, I controlled myself. Nancy listened intently as I told her about Daddy. Then I informed her I would be flying to Holland on Tuesday to be there in time for the funeral on Wednesday.

"Oh, you are going to the funeral?" she asked, sounding a little surprised.

"Nancy, he is my father!" I responded, not quite sure why it wouldn't be obvious to her that a daughter would want to attend the funeral of her beloved father.

A sudden heaviness filled my heart as I recalled the struggle I seemed to experience whenever I talked about Daddy. It felt like people in America and in Kenya didn't acknowledge my relationship to him as a daughter. Even though this relationship had started later in my life, and my adoption had never been formalized, for the last fifteen years Daddy had referred to me as nothing but his daughter. Since I had arrived in Holland for the first time in 1991, everyone I was introduced to knew me as part of the family—the daughter from Kenya. It is no wonder those in Holland had an easier time acknowledging the relationship. But even though I could understand that those who knew me in Kenya and in America might not appreciate this unique part of my life, it still hurt when questions were asked and the relationship was perceived as merely a friendship. He was my Daddy, and I wanted the world to know.

As Nancy hung up the phone, I recalled an incident that had occurred right after Steve and I had married. We had gone to his grandmother's home for Thanksgiving. In an effort to get to know some of the relatives, I had started a conversation with one of his aunts and, as usual, found myself answering questions about my history. As she asked if I had grown up in Kenya, I braced myself to answer questions so typical of Americans excited to be meeting an African for the first time. Dreading the inevitable drift of the conversation as it evolved into my life story, I glanced around the room in search of my husband. He was engaged in a different conversation, unable to rescue me.

"You had such a western wedding," she continued in a manner that left me wondering whether it was a question or a statement. *Here we go again*, I thought, feeling a little frustrated at the preconceived ideas about what is, or should be, African. My wedding had been similar to a typical wedding in Kenya, including a white dress, a veil, a tiered wedding cake, flowers, a few bridesmaids, and the Wedding March. Accustomed to western assumptions about my culture, I proceeded to respond with my usual tactfulness.

"Yes, if you count the number of westerners who were present. Otherwise, it really was similar to what I would have had at home." *Was that really tactful?*

"It's too bad nobody from your family could come to your wedding."

"Mommy and Daddy were there. Do you remember? They walked me down the aisle to give me away."

"Oh, it is nice to have such friends," she responded. My throat tightened as I struggled to find words to respond to her. Angered by her denial of my relationship to my parents, I smiled awkwardly and excused myself as I made my way toward my husband.

I went upstairs to find Seraiah's birth certificate for his passport application. Wondering why I had such a hard time convincing people that Daddy was really my father, memories of my relationship with him carried me back to my childhood days when he and his family were merely neighbors. Our family of five had lived happily close to their house with our mother Catherine Nyangweso, whom we fondly referred to as Mama. This memory of my childhood days took me back to when I was five years old.

Chapter 2
My Childhood

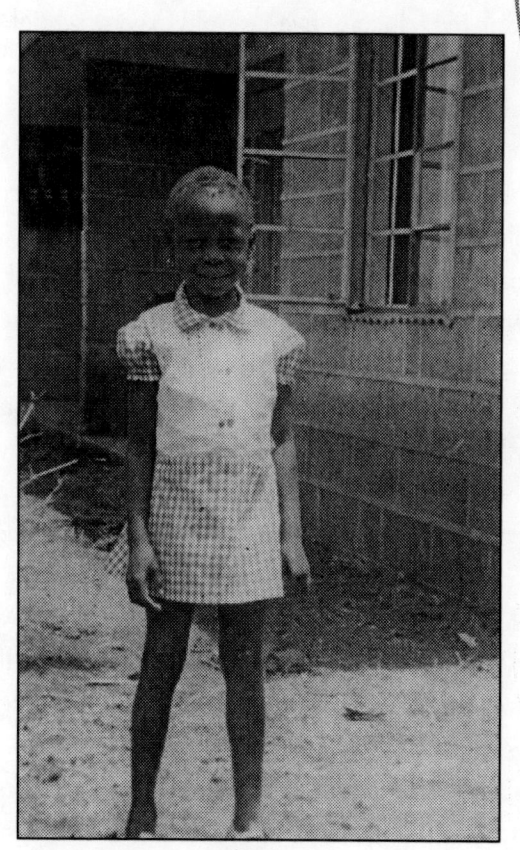

Susie

"I want to wear the white dress with little red squares and elastic and ribbons on the sleeves with a bow and…"

I described this imaginary dress to Mama as I tossed around in the bed I shared with her. She was frantically trying to get me ready for school, but I frustrated all her efforts by rejecting every dress she picked out for me to wear. Mama was quite accustomed to this daily routine of getting her reluctant five-year old to go to school. I had been eager to start school, simply wanting to imitate my brother David, four years older than I. He was my hero. From my earliest memories I had imitated him in everything he did. I wore his shorts, followed him around, and played with his friends in spite of his disapproval. When he started school, I read the books he read, used his pencils and paper, and talked like him. By the time I started school, I could read and write and knew my ABCs, which put me ahead of most of my classmates. What I found to be a boring daily routine, where kids just seemed to like playing silly games, made it hard to enjoy the school. *If only I could go to David's school…*

"Susie, you know very well you have no such dress," Mama spoke sternly, interrupting my thoughts. "We are going to be late. If you don't get dressed now I will have to spank you!" she continued, threatening me like she always did when I was behaving badly.

"Can I take some sugar then?" I asked, jumping out of bed to avoid the disciplinary measure Mama was good at delivering when necessary. I hated the porridge at break, so tasteless compared to what I was accustomed to at home.

"Yes, you can take some sugar. Just don't lick it all before you get to school." Mama hurriedly pulled off the slightly worn flannel nightdress I had inherited from our neighbors Wim and Margreet Bouw. They were missionaries from Holland and had been friends of our family for as long as I could remember. The Bouws frequently gave us hand-me-down clothing which we proudly wore. Of their five children, Pieter-Jan, Anne Marijke, Mirjam and David had been born in Kenya. Their eldest, Gisbert, was only a few months old when they came from Holland. Because I always seemed to be the recipient of clothes passed down from their children, I convinced myself that I, the youngest, was the most special.

I liked playing with the Bouw's kids, especially their middle child, Anne Marijke, who was six months younger than I. Perhaps it was because of this closeness in age that we were drawn to each other. Her younger sister, Mirjam, was just young enough to be annoying to kids our age. My brother played with the two older boys, Gisbert and Pieter-Jan. Their baby brother, David, was too young to play with any of us.

Margreet considered Mama her dear friend, and she spent her spare time visiting with Mama. She often brought us Dutch meals, when she prepared them.

Sometimes, when my brother David and I played at their house we ate meals there, too. They never seemed to mind.

Anne Marijke and I had our own adventures. One of our favorite games was to go shopping for our dolls in our own make believe store, buying all the toys, clothes, candy and other necessities that were dream items for any little girl, imagining how excited our dolls would be when we returned. We always played near their house. This way, Anne Marijke's mom wouldn't have to go far to find us when it was time for the mid-afternoon snack. I believed that I was part of Anne Marijke's family. It never seemed unusual to be included in their family activities. Wim and Margreet never made any distinction in the way they treated us. Often, Wim would take David and me, along with their kids, into town for ice cream. This was the best treat I could ever think of as a child. Mama knew I loved ice cream, but she didn't buy it often because of her limited resources. I never bothered her about it because, thanks to Wim, this need was adequately met.

"Can I have tea and bread spread with margarine?" I asked Mama as she continued to get me ready for school. She had picked out a green dress she had made me. While I loved the dress, it had a narrow neck that always felt tight when pulled over my head. This seemed to be true for most of my dresses, which made me hate getting ready in the morning. But this particular green dress was supposed to be special. Mama had sewed it by hand just for me. I loved the two large pockets, lightly embroidered in an intricate stitch, and low enough for my five-year old hands to rest in perfectly. Mama loved sewing.

"Yes, you can have tea and bread spread with margarine. But first, we need to get your face washed and get some lotion on you and comb your hair; then you can have your breakfast."

This daily ritual of getting ready for school was usually prolonged by my constant demand for explanations. I had an inquisitive mind and was never satisfied until all my questions were answered. Mama patiently answered each query, even though it was clear that her priority was to get us out of the house as quickly as possible. As soon as I was ready, I sat at the table to eat my breakfast as she got herself dressed. After breakfast, she took my hand and out the door we went.

Mama always walked the two mile journey to school with me. I knew the way so well that, even at that young age, I could have easily walked by myself. As a matter of fact, against Mama's approval, I quite often walked home as soon as the teacher released us for the morning break. Despite the fact that Mama would spank me and walk me back to school when I did this, I continued to make my escapes. I needed to cross a busy two-lane highway choked with trucks, buses and cars before walking the remainder of the two miles home. The danger was obvious to adults, but not to me.

I enjoyed the morning walks with Mama. It was a great opportunity for my inquiring mind to learn about all the things I needed to know. I can still remember the morning she explained why the Bouws lived in Kenya and not in their home in Holland. It was during one of those morning walks to school.

"Mama, why did the Bouws come to Kenya?" I asked soon after we crossed the road to walk on the same side as the traffic. Mama used to say that this way, if someone we knew was driving, he or she could easily stop to give us a lift.

"They came because they love Kenyan people and want to help them learn about Jesus." While the concept of missionary work was mind boggling for my young brain, I understood that it was sacrificial and entailed giving up the comfort of living in a home country, where life was much more convenient. Wim Bouw was the director of the Dutch Mission Center, where the Bouws and our family had lived for the first six years of my life. One of the goals of the Center, as everyone referred to it, was to train men and women to become leaders in the local congregations and to assist in community development projects. As is common with most mission bases, the missionaries built the Center using money from donors back in Holland, which meant that the missionaries' housing conditions were relatively more luxurious than those owned by local Kenyans. The Center had staff houses, recreational facilities, a church, dormitories for both men and women, and an administrative building equipped with offices, conference rooms, a kitchen, and a dining room.

We were fortunate to live in a relatively luxurious staff house built of stone, uncommon in the small farming town of Eldoret. Located on the western Rift Valley region of Kenya, this town was at the time predominantly populated by Kalenjin farmers who grew wheat for commercial purposes. They were also famous for keeping large herds of cattle for milk and beef.

"Remember to save your sugar for the porridge, OK?" Mama said, as we approached the school gates. Saying goodbye, she handed me the small plastic bag containing about two teaspoons of sugar. I had been using the excuse that the porridge at school was tasteless as a reason not to want to be at school, so I could escape from the boring activities I would have to endure there. All the other kids seemed to enjoy reciting the alphabet, which I was very familiar with, or playing silly games for babies, not "grown ups" like me. Mama started sending me with sugar, instead of letting me stay home as I had hoped. The sugar, however, didn't always make it to break time. I licked it or gave it away to the other kids and then still ran home before school was over.

I loved being at home. Even though Mama's matron job at the Center paid her just enough to buy our food, she had managed to make our house look beautiful. The living room had one old sofa (probably given to us by the Bouws) two armchairs, four stools, and a small table in the center of the room. Mama had embroidered some tablecloths, which she proudly laid on the table and on the arms of the sofa. At one end of the room was a small cupboard where Mama kept her most precious cups and saucers, water glasses and plates, and above it was a clock, which chimed every hour, conveniently telling us the time of day or night.

On top of the cupboard was an embroidered runner with a beautiful china tea set, which Mama had received as a wedding gift. One day, as I was going about my usual mischief, in an attempt to discover what the set really looked like, I pulled the runner off the cupboard. The precious china tea set came crashing down with a sound that brought Mama running from the kitchen to see what I had done this time. I can still remember the shock on her face as she spoke the words I was so used to hearing:

"What have you done?" After staring at me with her accusing eyes for what seemed like eternity, she bent down and looked through the pile of broken pieces to see if any of the china had survived the crash.

I retreated toward the wall in fear of the punishment that would befall me.

My voice broke as I apologized profusely, and started to cry. The tears seemed to work their magic, for as soon as the first few drops hit the floor, she abandoned her efforts to recover any unbroken pieces and comforted me. Mama was always forgiving whenever accidents happened, but it never stopped me from being scared when I thought I was in trouble. As she wiped my face and encouraged me to be careful, I nodded and stuck my left index and middle fingers into my mouth.

Close to the cupboard was another table that held our only source of entertainment, a Phillips radio. Mama's brother, Eliud, had bought it for us, claiming that he wanted to keep up with the news whenever he visited. Every night after supper, our family would sit in the living room and listen to the radio while we chatted. With the radio playing in the background, we loved to hear Mama tell stories about her life. She had been born in a place called Bukura, a sublocation of Kakamega, in western Kenya where her parents still lived. Mama was the second born in a family of six. Three of her sisters lived at home in Bukura with Grandma and Grandpa, while her brother Eliud and her sister Agnes lived in Nairobi, the capital city of Kenya.

Mama had attended a teacher training college and had taught at different primary schools before taking her job as matron at the Center. During her career as a teacher, Mama had endured many transfers, and had dragged all of her children along. She often told a story about a night when she was traveling to yet another school, with five of us tagging along. Transport in those days was very unreliable. The bus had stopped in the middle of nowhere and the driver, without offering any explanation, had announced that the bus wouldn't be going any further.

"What happened to us?" I had asked curiously as she told the story. My finger was temporarily removed from my mouth as I climbed onto her lap to hear her better. I loved sitting on Mama's lap. It made me feel safe and special. Resuming my finger sucking, I listened intently as Mama told the story.

"When the bus pulled away, all the other passengers walked off, and we were left on the side of the road," Mama explained.

"We really got scared, but Mama was not afraid," Lydia, my eldest sister volunteered, looking up from a book she was reading.

"I didn't know where we were but I needed to be strong because you were all depending on me," Mama continued.

"What did you do then?" I asked impatiently.

"As the five of you huddled together in the cold, dark, still air, I quietly prayed and asked God to send us help."

"Did God send help?" I asked unable to contain my curiosity.

"Margy noticed a shop not too far from where we were. We walked toward the shop hoping someone could at least let us stay the night."

I glanced over to Margy, who was now smiling proudly as Mama told about her discovery. Margy continued the story.

"The store owner opened the door after we knocked twice, and when Mama told him what had happened, he let us stay the night in the house behind the shop." Margy always went straight to the point when she talked. In my mind I visualized a tall man with a smiley face, a little like Uncle Eliud, opening the door and letting us into a warm, cozy house where he served us a warm cup of milky tea.

"Did he make us tea?" I asked hoping Mama would say yes.

"No, it was late at night and the rest of the man's family had gone to bed." Although Mama's response was a little disappointing, I still enjoyed listening to stories about our adventures as a family. Whenever Mama told stories like this, she always reminded us that God, in whom she trusted, had always provided for us.

I enjoyed the closeness my family shared, even with such diverse personalities. Lydia, my eldest sister, was the quiet one in the family. Her nickname was "The Passive One." True to her nickname, Lydia never seemed to respond to any of the commotion typical in a house full of children. But, despite her lack of physical responsiveness to her surroundings, she loved school and books. Her love for books was evident in her performance at school. Mama was proud of Lydia's academic excellence and always said she would one day be a doctor, the most highly respected profession in Kenya at the time.

The second born, Judy, had the nickname "Pack and Go." She always seemed to be going somewhere. At seventeen, in addition to her endless expeditions, she had developed a very particular taste in fashion, which my brother David considered to be ridiculous. I remember one Saturday afternoon when she was getting ready for one of her explorations, and the two of them got into a fight. On that particular Saturday, she was taking an unusually long time in getting ready and became frustrated when she could not find the pair of trousers she had laid out to wear. As it turned out, David had hidden the pair in the wooden suitcase under his bed, claiming that trousers were not meant for girls. As always, Mama had to intervene by pulling Judy away from David.

Margy was a typical middle child. Unable to fit in with the two older ones or my brother and me, she developed ways to get attention from Mama. Her way seemed to always involve my feelings being wounded. When she wasn't calling me names or pulling my fingers out of my mouth, she would be sneering or making faces at me. She got into trouble on my account several times a day. Her nickname was "The Wild One," but I preferred to think of her as "The Bully."

Although it was evident that Mama had very limited means to support her family, she never seemed to despair. In fact, she often called us "the royal family" and took pride in simple things, like the clothes she made for us by hand and the cakes she occasionally baked. When we sat in the living room to talk and listen to the radio in the evenings, Mama reminded us that we were blessed to enjoy such family times, because there were children who did not have this privilege. Her faith in God was unwavering. Whenever she had a need, she always called the family together and prayed that God would meet the need in His own way. As a child, even though I didn't understand much about this faith, I felt comforted by Mama's source of strength.

Mama's role as a matron was to maintain the Center's administrative facility, with responsibilities ranging from keeping it clean to event planning. Our family seemed to eat at the Center's dining room a lot. Since Mama was also responsible for dispensing the meals served at events, she always knew when there would be leftovers. These, along with the occasional meals provided by the Bouws, enabled our family to maintain a stable, healthy diet. The healthy part, however, only applied to everyone else in the family. I was not much of an eater and was known to prefer only tea and bread, in addition to the occasional ice cream supplied by the Bouws.

Mama would clean up the tables after serving the residents, then proceed to set a table for our family. As a child, eating at the Center's dining room seemed very natural to me, since Mama spent most of her days at this building. While the rest of the family enjoyed their meal, my favorite activity would be to see how many tables I could walk on without stepping down. I would ignore Mama's orders to stop playing on the tables. After my family was done eating, the tables were cleaned, and the dishes washed and put away, as if on cue I would suddenly become hungry and in need of tea with bread and margarine.

For Mama and my sisters who were old enough to help around the house, preparing my "special diet" meant that once we went back home someone would have to prepare the tea, which was not a quick process in itself. If there was no bread at home, someone would also have to go buy some. Fortunately, the shops were not too far from the house. The process of preparing the tea consisted of heating milk and water almost to boiling and then adding tea leaves. At that point, the temperature needed to be lowered to allow the tea to brew before completely boiling. Then one had to quickly remove it from the heat before it flowed over; which meant someone had to stand there and watch it. My sisters can swear that a watched teapot never boils.

My perfect cup of tea consisted of half water and half milk. And the tea leaves had to be just right, giving the tea a light caramel color. In the meantime, the bread had to be spread with margarine. I never understood why my sisters made such a fuss about my eating habits. In their opinion, nothing was ever quite right with me. The tea was either too hot or too cold. There was no pleasing me.

My Childhood

In spite of our family feuds, we loved spending time together. But we were not the only ones who enjoyed being with Mama. She and Margreet spent a lot of time together. The two were members of a women's group that met frequently to discuss different issues relating to the family, and women's roles in society. Mama was the chairwoman of this group. I enjoyed accompanying her to the meetings because they always served tea. One afternoon, after everyone had finished drinking their tea, I'd gone around the room taking any cup I could reach and draining any leftovers. Mama had noticed this just about the time everyone else did. There were roars of laughter as Mama quickly took me and sat me on her lap and firmly told me to never do that again. When Mama related this story to my sisters, they had laughed at me until Mama stopped them, the embarrassment almost sending me to tears.

Neighbors also enjoyed listening to Mama's stories. They always seemed to stop by just to visit with her. During those visits, they would laugh as Mama told stories about life at the Center. She was loved by many who knew her. Neighbors referred to her as the joyful one. She was always smiling or singing wherever she was. She frequently told jokes and laughed animatedly as she did so, slapping her right hip several times as if to emphasize how funny the jokes were. Mama's laugh exposed a gap between her two front teeth, which she had insisted was a sign of beauty among the Luhya people. Women from some of the other tribes would argue that their own version of beauty, defined by attributes such as long necks or fat legs, was more attractive. I would listen intently and form my own opinion, which was always in favor of Mama's opinion.

There were times when Mama would send me to go play with my brother David, arguing that I needed to leave the adults alone. David, for the most part, looked after me whenever we were out playing with his numerous friends. He was the one who listened to me when I complained about a three-legged dog that always seemed to follow me at school. The dog had been born with four legs, but one hind leg had been through some trauma that left it slightly shorter than the others, giving the dog an interesting hop. Why this dog seemed to always come in my direction, I never could understand. Mama highly doubted that the dog existed. It wasn't until one of my schoolmates confirmed the existence of the three-legged dog that Mama finally believed it wasn't just a story.

David's affection was not always disposed in my favor, like the time when he kept throwing sticks at me because I was following him. He and his friends were working on some interesting project I wasn't allowed to see. They were actually constructing carts using sticks cut from the trees in the nearby wooded area and nails that my brother had bought.

"Where did you get the money?" I had asked as soon as I learned he had bought the nails.

My Childhood

"Go back home!" David had ordered me.

I insisted on asking about the source of the money, until one of the boys revealed that David had stolen it.

I looked at David in disbelief. When he made no attempt to deny the allegation, my mouth dropped in utter shock. Mama would be very upset. I could not believe my brother would do such a horrible thing, nor imagine the kind of consequence he would have to face when Mama found out. I was afraid for David, yet I felt a sense of obligation to inform Mama. Without any further discussion, I turned around and ran as fast as I could to the Center. Entering through the wide double doors at the front, I rushed passed the reception area and headed for the kitchen where I knew I'd find Mama. She was accustomed to my getting excited over the most trivial events, so when she saw the state I was in, she was hardly alarmed. But when I told her what had happened, she was outraged and demanded that I ask David to come home immediately. This was the first time any of her children had done anything like this. David got a really good spanking that day.

Even though my relationship with David at times seemed to depend on his mood and his company, I wished I attended his school, so I could play with him. At the end of the first term at school, I was pleasantly surprised and overjoyed to learn that Mama had talked to the headmaster at David's school about interviewing me so I could be considered for a late entry to standard one. At last Mama understood me! In my mind I began to visualize all the different learning activities that would soon become part of my life, as opposed to the boring alphabet drills I endured each day. The first day at the new school couldn't come soon enough.

The interview with the headmaster a few weeks later went well, according to Mama. All I remember from the process was that I had to put my right arm over my head to touch my left ear, and this ability to touch the tip of my ear qualified me for entry into standard one. Six was the right age for entry at this level, but since I was still five, I had needed to demonstrate my preparedness. Mama said I had answered all the questions with great confidence. When my first day at the new school came, it was with great poise that I walked into the building.

"Good morning class!" bellowed the large woman standing at the front of the crowded classroom. There were a few moments of continued commotion as children rushed to take their seats. It was my first day at Sosiani Primary School. I was now in standard one. That morning, Mama had had an easy time getting me ready as she dressed me in the white blouse, maroon tunic, white socks and black shoes: the official uniform for this school.

"Good morning madam!" the children responded in unison. They were obviously familiar with the routine. This being the second term of the school year, they had at least three months of experience over me. I looked around the room to see if I recognized any of the other children. Surprisingly, they didn't seem to notice I was new. Even if they did, they didn't show it. But the teacher knew, and chose to inform the rest of the class at that precise moment.

"We have a new pupil with us today," she announced, looking in my direction. Since I was sitting in the front row, I turned around to make sure all the other children took a good look at me. This self-confident attribute had been shaped by Mama's belief in me. She always seemed to be easily impressed by everything I did. My sister, Margy, tells the story of a picture I once drew, which apparently resembled a map. I don't remember thinking about maps, or even understanding their function in life, but, according to Margy, as soon as the picture was complete Mama had asked what the picture was. I had confidently replied: "It's a map." To this Mama responded with abundant praise and declared that I would someday be an artist.

"What is your name?" the teacher asked in a gentle voice that surprised me, since her greeting earlier had scared some of the children. It seemed appropriate to stand before answering this question. Once on my feet, I looked straight into the teacher's eyes and replied:

"Susie Awinja." The teacher thanked me and asked me to sit.

Without further ado, the teacher proceeded to announce the lesson of the day, which was to be about our families. This sounded very exciting to me, since I thoroughly enjoyed every aspect of my family. She ordered us to have our pencils and exercise books ready for a writing activity. This was getting even more exciting by the minute. I had waited the whole of April school holidays to write in my new ruled, 32-page exercise book used in primary schools. While the pencil wasn't new to me, most of my writing and drawing activities had been on single sheets of paper that Mama borrowed from my brother when he wouldn't share with me. While I was just beginning to get lost in thoughts about my wonderful family, I was interrupted by the teacher's instruction for our first activity.

"Write down your father's name."

Father? I asked myself, not sure I understood what she was asking us to do. For the next several minutes, countless questions ran through my mind. *Who is my father? Do I have a father?* I pondered these thoughts, wondering if the other kids were asking the same questions. As I looked around, most of them were busy writing. *Does everyone have a father?* Several images of the men I knew went through my mind. *Why couldn't she have asked us to write our mother's name? That would have been easy: Catherine Nyangwesò.* I knew Mama's name and could spell it correctly. But the idea of having my own father was a concept I had never considered before.

My Childhood

Could it be my uncle Eliud Amayayi? Eliud was Mama's brother who visited us often, a warm and loving man who brought me something special whenever he visited. Based on my observation of our neighbor Wim, I knew fathers were nice people. They loved their children and often bought them special gifts, just like Wim did. Uncle Eliud had demonstrated this same attribute whenever he came. Determined not to run out of time, I quickly wrote, "My father's name is Eliud Amayayi." I put the pencil down in satisfaction and waited for the next activity.

By the time class ended at noon, the issue of fathers was still unresolved. Although the teacher had not questioned my answer, somewhere, at the back of my mind, I needed to know who my father was. Mama was waiting for me at the school's gate. While the plan had been that my brother David would walk home with me, Mama wanted to be the one to pick me up on the first day. I ran toward her the moment I caught sight of her. Flinging myself into her waiting arms, I began to babble about my new teacher, realizing as I did so that I had no idea what her name was. I knew from my experience at my previous school that "madam" was merely a title. But I'd been so busy soaking in everything about standard one that I hadn't stopped to consider asking what my teacher's name was.

For lunch Mama had prepared a simple meal consisting of maize and beans boiled together until they were soft enough to chew. She served this with a warm cup of milky tea, just the way I liked it. By now I was beginning to outgrow my unhealthy eating practices and was gradually becoming more tolerant of the foods the rest of the family enjoyed. But I had not outgrown my finger sucking habit. Mama had tried every trick she knew, including lacing my fingers with hot pepper, but nothing seemed to work. She would even threaten that if I didn't stop, one day the two fingers, which looked just a little thinner than the rest due to the continued sucking, would disappear altogether. I reasoned that, until then, they were still there to be enjoyed.

Halfway through the meal, I popped the question that had been plaguing me since the first activity at school:

"Who is my father?"

Mama froze, her spoon somewhere between her mouth and her plate. Had she not understood the question? Just as I was about to ask again, she recovered and gently placed her left hand over my right hand. With her eyes looking into mine, she said delicately:

"Your father died a long time ago." I understood there was more to this story, but that I was not to ask further questions. For the remainder of the term, I focused on all the new subjects I was learning, and as Mama continued to pour out her endless love, there was no reason to dwell on the issue of my father.

Joining David's school was not the only change in our home. When Lydia and Judy completed their primary education at standard seven, Mama had managed to send them to boarding school. Since David and I were still young, Margy was the one Mama called upon to help with the daily chores. She came home at one o'clock every afternoon during her lunch break. After lunch, she would clean the dishes while Mama rushed back to work. Just before two, Margy would run back to school. David and I would then spend the afternoon playing together. Weeks turned into months and in January, the start of the new school year, I transitioned into standard two. April school holidays approached again and we looked forward to the break because Lydia and Judy would be coming home. When they arrived, Mama surprised us with the most exciting news:

"Who wants to go to Nairobi?" Mama asked, holding a letter she had received earlier.

"Me! Me!" I screamed in excitement.

David came to the living room where the rest of us were sitting after returning from the evening meal at the Center. We had quickly settled back into our usual routine of staying up late talking, while listening to the radio.

"What for?" Judy asked in a skeptical tone.

"Well, do you want to go or not?" Mama asked again, teasing.

"Who is the letter from?" Margy asked, trying to snatch the letter. Mama raised her hand, holding the letter higher so Margy couldn't reach it.

"Aunt Josephine is getting married and we are attending her wedding," Lydia announced, spoiling the fun of guessing as usual.

"And you, Lydia, are a bridesmaid," Mama added as she handed Margy the letter.

We gathered around the table and prompted Mama to tell us more about the wedding. It was to take place on April sixth so we only had a few days to get ready. As we talked into the night, plans to attend the wedding continued to unfold. Afterward, Judy and Lydia told stories about their schools, and the rest of us shared about all that had happened while they were away. Life at my new school had continued to be all I ever dreamed it would be. At the end of the term, I had ranked second in my class. Mama proudly shared this news with Lydia and Judy since they had not been there when I'd brought my report card home. The two terms before that I had ranked seventh, so this had been a great improvement. David was doing very well, too. In fact, all of us were excellent students.

On Thursday, April 4, we made the four-hour bus trip to Nairobi. Aunt Josephine picked us up from the bus station and took us to her little house west of the city center. After settling us in, she brought out Lydia's bridesmaid's dress. It was a beautiful, long pink dress, with lace across the bodice and a zipper on the back. I wished I was Lydia. I couldn't wait to see her in it.

As soon as she tried it on, we all screamed as she walked back into the living room to show off. She looked like a princess. We spent most of that evening and Friday preparing for the wedding and touring the city. I had never before visited Nairobi, the capital city of Kenya, and it was much busier than I expected. The buildings were taller than any I'd ever seen, and people on the streets seemed to be in a great hurry. The shops were bigger than the ones in Eldoret, and ice cream seemed to be sold on every corner. Since ice cream was my favorite treat, I stared through the large windows as we passed, ignoring the faces that stared back. I wondered if Mama would be able to buy me some.

When she offered to indulge us in this favorite treat I was ecstatic. Inside the ice cream parlor we each picked out a favorite, mine being a vanilla cone. Slowly licking it to enjoy it for as long as possible, I thought about the times Wim Bouw had taken us for similar treats. I couldn't wait to tell Anne Marijke about the experience.

Chapter 3

The End of My Childhood

The night we arrived back in Eldoret, Mama had a strange dream. In it she was wearing a white dress, a color women wore at funerals. She was looking down at her own body lying in a coffin. If the dream bothered Mama, she never showed it. But to Lydia, who had become interested in spiritual matters since joining N'giya Girls High School the previous term, the implication of such a dream was troubling. Mama dismissed any concerns Lydia raised, claiming nothing was going to happen, and if it did, there was nothing we could do. In the days following, Lydia had her own premonition that something bad would happen to her. Being the eldest, she knew it would break Mama's heart if she were to die, so she prayed God would spare Mama such heartache.

Mama was enjoying having her older daughters home during the school break, since they helped with most of the household chores. I was growing quickly and eager to be like my sisters. I even wanted earrings. All my sisters wore earrings, so I told Mama I wanted them too. She told me I would need to have my ears pierced, and that might hurt. I determined to do whatever it took just to be like my sisters. So the day for my ears to be pierced came, and I endured the pain. My brother made fun of me as usual, so I cried, but life went on as normal.

As the end of the holidays drew closer, Lydia and Judy prepared to return to their schools. Mama always did some minor shopping for my sisters, buying them necessities such as soap and toothpaste before they left for school. Everyone understood that she couldn't buy new clothes or other luxuries all the time. This particular time, however, she extended herself beyond everyone's expectation. She bought Lydia and Judy shoes, clothes and handbags. Judy, who tended to be sensitive about money matters, questioned Mama and stated that she personally didn't need some of the items. But Mama insisted.

The day before Judy and Lydia left, Mama asked a local photographer to come and take a family picture. While we didn't have photos taken often, I enjoyed the process and liked the final product even better. My earliest memory of picture taking had been a year before that on my fifth birthday. I hadn't understood the concept

The End of My Childhood

of picture taking, especially because the word used in Luhya to describe the process translated to a person being "beaten a picture." To my surprise, the process had ended up being so painless that I was disappointed.

Monday morning came quickly. Margy's school was starting that day, so she woke up early. Mama took the day off so she could help Lydia and Judy prepare for their departure later. It was also a good chance for her to take some time off, because later in the week there was going to be a big conference at the Center, which meant she would have more work than usual.

When the time came for Lydia and Judy to leave, David, Mama and I accompanied the two of them to the bus station to say goodbye. Since they were going in different directions, they were to take separate buses. Holding Lydia's and Judy's hands, I walked between them as we moved toward the first bus, which was going to Judy's school. Mama handed the bus conductor Judy's luggage.

"Take good care of that suitcase," Mama instructed.

As Judy got on the bus, Mama reminded her to write as soon as she arrived.

We then went to Lydia's bus and performed the same ritual. As soon as Lydia was getting on the bus, Margy came running, so the goodbyes started all over again.

Mama then went back and forth between Lydia's and Judy's buses bidding them farewell. When she went back to Lydia's bus for the sixth time, Lydia started to cry.

"Mama, what is wrong?" she asked in between sobs. "Why are you saying goodbye so many times?" she continued. "Does this have anything to do with the dream you had two weeks ago?"

"Don't be silly," Mama had responded. She then said one final goodbye to the two and joined us as we waited for the buses to take off. We waved as they slowly pulled away, Lydia's bus heading southwest toward Kisumu and Judy's heading northwest toward Kitale. While I missed my sisters very much when they were at school, Mama's constant presence provided a sense of stability that gave me an unshakable security, regardless of all the changes around me.

Mama went to work the following day and worked long hours for two days. On Wednesday night, after her second long day, she went to bed early. I always went to bed as soon as she did. That night, Mama seemed a little distraught. She could not fall asleep, so she took a hymnal and started to sing some of her favorite songs. In between singing, she read verses from the Bible. Mama loved the Bible. She often recited verses and encouraged us to memorize passages. Right after our return from Nairobi, she had written on a large piece of blue construction paper Psalm 27:4 which says, "One thing I ask of the Lord, this is what I seek: that I may dwell in the house of the Lord all the days of my life, to gaze upon the beauty of the Lord and to seek Him in His temple."

The End of My Childhood

That night, Mama continued to sing even after I fell asleep. I awoke a few times to complain about the light, but she continued to praise and worship, assuring me that it wouldn't be long before she, too, fell asleep. The following morning she woke me up in a rather unusual manner, asking if I would get out of bed. She needed to straighten it out and lie down for a little while, as she was not feeling well. The sun was already up and Margy had left for school.

"Breakfast is ready. Just ask David to help you with it, OK?" she had said.

After breakfast, David left to go play with his friends. I stayed home, wanting to be close to Mama just in case she needed me. I went back to the bedroom to see how she was doing. Her breathing was laborious, and as I watched her chest move up and down, a cold chill ran down my spine. I had never seen Mama look so helpless. I knew whatever she was suffering from must be serious, and I feared she might never get better. I moved closer to the bed and sat down beside her, placing my head next to her face. The pillow underneath her head was drenched with sweat. I quickly went to the bathroom, took a wash cloth, and ran some water on it to soak it, just as I had seen her do whenever one of us was sick. Then, as I began to gently wipe her face, she attempted to smile and slowly pulled me close. Still holding the wash cloth, I snuggled next to her, wanting to be near, with the hope that my presence would comfort her. As

I lay still beside her, I could hear the clock in the living room ticking, synchronized with Mama's heartbeat.

As the clock chimed eleven, Mama turned toward me and, struggling to communicate, she managed to whisper, "Please go to the Center…and see…if anyone could take me to the hospital."

Without wasting a moment, I ran out the door heading straight for Mwangi, the office messenger who was enjoying his mid-morning tea in the dining area. Mwangi dashed into the office. A few minutes later he came out accompanied by the Center's driver. As the driver went to get the car ready, Mwangi and I ran back to our house.

I packed some clothes for Mama as we waited for the car. As soon as the driver came, the two men helped Mama into the car. Because of her grave condition, Mwangi suggested they take her to Plateau, a Dutch Church mission hospital 45 kilometers away. In spite of the great distance, it was considered better than the closer District General hospital. I was afraid of hospitals because of all the shots I had received during my visits. I was already apprehensive about accompanying Mama, much as I wanted to be with her. As I brought her clothes to the car, I determined to stay behind and handed the bag with Mama's clothes to Mwangi.

"Susie, please come with me," Mama begged me as she tried to lift herself up from the backseat where Mwangi and the driver had laid her. She knew about

The End of My Childhood

my fears and tried to convince me that all would be well. Unable to express my feelings, I shook my head and retreated to the wall by the bedroom window, near where the car was parked. Mama's continued plea only made me feel worse as guilt began to set in. I was torn between the desire to cling to my dear Mama, who looked frighteningly sicker than I had ever seen anyone, and the need to protect myself from the unknown mysteries of the hospital world. A part of me wanted her to come and scoop me in her arms like she always did whenever I was being defiant. I felt angry with her for being sick. *Make me come with you!* I thought. My overwhelming emotions drowned the world around me, and I could see only her moving lips. I could hardly hear what she was saying, and as tears ran down my face, I shook my head profusely—not because I was saying no to her plea, but because I desperately wanted everything to stop. I had had enough. I wanted Mama to be well. I wanted her right by me like always.

Through my tear-filled eyes, I watched Mwangi get in the car and slowly pull away. Everything seemed to happen in slow motion. As the brake lights turned on, I took one step forward, then another. The car jerked back in reverse. Had the driver seen me? I rushed forward, hoping to let Mwangi know I wanted to come. The car started to move just as I approached the passenger's side. I called out to Mama in desperation as it became clear that the car was gaining speed and leaving me behind.

"Noooooooo!!!!" I screamed.

As the car sped toward the gate, the left signal started blinking, and the driver waited for traffic to clear. I continued to run after them. As they turned left to merge onto Kisumu road, I knew I was too late.

I sat on the ground and kicked my legs back and forth as I screamed, "Mama." David, who heard from a neighbor that Mama had been taken to the hospital, came to the gate where I was crying uncontrollably. He tried to comfort me, but all I wanted was Mama. Unable to help me, he ran back to the house and called our neighbor, who came and carried me home.

When Margy came back at one o'clock, she was surprised to learn about Mama's sudden illness. She prepared lunch but we couldn't eat—not with Mama away at the hospital. After nibbling on the food, I convinced Margy we should all go back to the gate and wait for Mama. The three of us sat and watched cars drive by. To cheer us up, Margy started playing "I Spy." She would yell out a car color and we would try and spot it. But all the while, as we counted red and white cars, I kept looking out for the one that had taken Mama away. After what seemed like a really long time, I finally saw it.

"There they are!" I shouted jumping up and down.

The car slowed down to pull in at the Center's entrance. Recognizing us, the driver slowed down and stopped. Mama wasn't in the car. Instead, Mwangi came

The End of My Childhood

out of the car and walked toward us, holding the bag I'd packed Mama's clothes in. It seemed just as full as before. As Mwangi handed the bag to Margy, the significance of this single act was obvious. I turned toward Margy and, without hesitation, said "Mama is dead."

Chapter 4
DIVIDING THE FIVE

From left: Margy, David, Judy, Susie and Lydia

He Really Is My Father

"**M**ama is dead!" I shouted in misery as Margy took the bag of clothes from Mwangi.

"Don't say that. She is not dead," Margy replied sternly.

Mwangi, still standing nearby, simply looked at Margy, as if to give her time to ask any questions she might have.

"How is she?" Margy asked after a long pause. Mwangi did not answer. Instead, he asked for directions to where Grandma lived.

Margy took David and me to the house, gave us instructions to stay close by, and told us that everything was going to be just fine. I wished Wim and Margreet were with us. Even though the concept of a father was still unclear to me, I had come to look up to Wim like a father. He was kind and enjoyed playing with my brother and me. One of my favorite games with him was going around in circles between his legs. I'd see him in the hallway at the Center, or even outside the buildings, and if he happened to be standing still, perhaps in a conversation with someone, that would be my opportunity. I would sneak up to him, place my hand around his knee, and begin to go around circling first one leg, then the next several times. I would continue until Wim would bend down and pick me up saying, "I got you!" We would both laugh, as he tickled me and I kicked, until he put me down.

Dividing the Five

If only Wim were here. After Margy and Mwangi left for Grandma's house in Bukura, David and I sat outside, so sad that we wouldn't bring ourselves to play. We hardly said a word to each other. We just sat there, each consumed by a quiet we'd never experienced before. For once David did not tease me. Somehow I wished he would. I wished Mama would come back. I desperately wanted her back. But instead of my dear Mama, our neighbor came to check on us. Later she fed us a meal that to me was without taste, because all I wanted was Mama. After dinner, I went to bed and tried to sleep on my own, something I had never done before. The accumulated exhaustion from all that had happened that day finally gave way to a deep sleep.

I woke up later that night to sounds of wailing. I stepped out of bed and made my way to the living room, which was now crowded with relatives from Mama's side.

Fingers in my mouth, I looked around the room in search of Margy. To my surprise, Lydia and Judy were already at the house. I ran across the room to Lydia and raised my arms toward her. She took the cue and picked me up. My presence in the room seemed to increase the wailing.

"This poor little child," I heard someone say.

"Oh my child," Grandma and Grandpa chanted simultaneously as they wailed. I barely understood death, but I knew it meant I couldn't be with Mama, and everyone was upset about it. The crying continued all night, combined with whispers as the newcomers asked for details of all that had happened. Having been the only one at home when Mama fell ill, I felt like a small hero. Everyone would look at me and then pose the same question that all were asking: "Was she the only one at home?" This would be followed by the explanation that I had called for help. The envy-filled looks I received made me feel like I had had the unique privilege that most wished they had—to have spent the last moments of Mama's life with her.

"What's going to happen to the five of them?" someone asked.

I had not considered this. Turning to Lydia, I asked in a loud whisper: "Are you going to be our new Mama?" Lydia broke into tears and the wailing started all over again.

A few minutes later, there was some commotion from outside and a few of the people sitting closest to the door stood up and moved to make room for some new arrivals. Among them was my favorite uncle.

"Uncle Eliud!" I exclaimed as I wiggled in Lydia's arms to let her know I wanted to be put down. I started to walk toward him, but halfway across the room I suddenly stopped at the sound of a crash. Overwhelmed by the grief of Mama's death, Uncle Eliud had picked up our Philips radio and thrown it down, sending it crashing onto the concrete floor. Some of the women went to comfort him. Realizing that he wouldn't hold me, I turned around and ran back to Lydia.

The following day, neighbors came and offered their condolences, as the five of us huddled together in the living room where we had spent so many evenings with Mama. It felt wrong to be there without her. Earlier that morning, we had been taken to the hospital to see her body. As I had looked at her limp figure underneath the hospital sheets, a sense of guilt overwhelmed me as I remembered how I had refused to accompany her to the hospital. *Did she know that I had changed my mind and tried to come?*

On Saturday, Mama's body was brought to our house for one last time before being transported home to Bukura for burial. She lay so peacefully with her arms across her chest in the wooden coffin that rested on the table in our living room. I asked to sit on a chair next to the coffin. As people came in to pay their last respects, I stared at Mama, wondering if she would smile to acknowledge them just like she had always done. The Bouws were among those who came to our house that day. They found out about Mama's death when they returned from their vacation in Mombasa. Margreet was overcome with grief and cried uncontrollably for several minutes as she stood by the coffin. She picked me up and held me close. She and Wim stayed at our house for the remainder of that day and helped serve food to the funeral guests. Later that evening, Wim accompanied the five of us as we transported Mama's body home, where she was buried the following Monday.

After the funeral we returned to Eldoret, and the next few days were spent going through Mama's things and sorting them. Some of our aunts helped themselves to Mama's clothes. Aunt Agnes, whom I had only just met at the funeral, took most of our belongings. She helped herself to bedding, kitchen utensils, furniture, and other small items. All these were loaded into a lorry outside the house. As I followed Lydia around, the same way I used to follow Mama, I tried to process all that was happening. It was becoming clear to me that we were not going to be living at the house anymore, judging by how empty it looked.

"Let's take these to the Bouws," Lydia said, holding a pile of papers. I followed her to the Bouw's house, excited at the prospect of seeing Anne Marijke. Margreet, seeing us through her kitchen window, opened the door to let us in. She picked me up, held me close and attempted a greeting, but instead she burst into tears and cried for several minutes. Lydia, still holding the pile of papers, started to cry, too.

"These are for you," she finally said as she wiped her tears and handed the papers to Margreet, explaining they were from Mama's women's group. Margreet then offered us some tea. We sat at the very table Mama had sat at with Margreet merely two weeks before her death. Mama had been extremely concerned about our well-being and had asked if Margreet would pray with her for us children. Was it possible that Mama was somehow being prepared for all that was to happen? As Margreet and Lydia talked about the shock of this sudden death, Margreet mentioned that she and Wim were considering adopting the five of us. They agreed that it would be best to discuss this with our relatives. I later learned that the idea had been rejected on the basis of the fact that our relatives were capable of taking care of us, which was the only explanation that was given to me as I became separated from my family.

Aunt Agnes led me to the back seat of a long grey Zephyr, where she sat next to me as Lydia, Judy, Margy and David waved goodbye. Uncle Gideon, whom I presumed to be Aunt Agnes' husband, started to drive the Zephyr away as I desperately tried to read the looks on the faces of my brother and sisters. Did they approve of this? Desperate, I rolled down the window and called out to Lydia. Aunt Agnes then pulled me back down, saying everything would be okay.

"Let me stay with them!" I demanded as she closed the window. I turned around in my seat to look back. David and Judy were still waving.

"Please, let me go back!" This time I begged, thinking my politeness would make a difference. Uncle Gideon continued to drive while Aunt Agnes simply looked at me. I turned around again to look at my family. They were quickly vanishing from my view as we approached the Center's entrance, perhaps for the last time. I was frightened by this thought. Where was I being taken? Would I ever see my family again? Would the four of them stay together or be divided? As we merged onto Kisumu road, I angrily slumped into my seat and turned around to face the side window. Losing Mama was painful. But to have my family ripped from me on purpose was more than I could bear. As I wrestled with this, I never once looked at Aunt Agnes who had by now placed her arm over my shoulders. How could they do this to me?

Chapter 5

Shock to the System

"Buy banana for the child, please buy banana for the child. Toto, are you hungry?" called the distant voices, as I squirmed in my seat trying to get comfortable.

"Eggs for sale, eggs for sale…" The voices got louder. I opened my eyes, and blinked several times as the bright sunlight shone through the window and onto my face. The car had stopped. I looked around to see the source of the voices. Exhausted, I rubbed my eyes and yawned, struggling to wake up from my tired sleep.

"Cover your mouth!" Aunt Agnes' voice emerged from the front seat, startling me. I closed my mouth promptly and looked at her, shocked by her words. As our eyes locked, her disapproving stare caused me to look down in shame.

Slowly, I began to recall the events leading to my being confined in the back seat of this car. I must have fallen asleep soon after we left Eldoret earlier that day. The last thing I remembered was Aunt Agnes placing her arm over my shoulders in an attempt to comfort me. She must have moved to the front seat while I was sleeping.

Uncle Gideon was presently not in the car, and I assumed he had gone to use the restroom. Only a few weeks earlier we had stopped at this same rest stop on our way to Nairobi for Aunt Josephine's wedding. Mama had cautioned us against eating any of the foods sold by the vendors, claiming they were not always fresh and could lead to upset stomachs.

A lump formed in my throat as I looked back on the recent events and just how alive Mama had been. I swallowed hard to prevent myself from crying. I glanced at Aunt Agnes again, trying to read her mood. Mama had always been gentle with me. Whenever I'd done something wrong, she had disciplined me, but I always understood what my wrongdoing was. I was certain that she would not have interpreted failure to cover my mouth as a wrong. She would have gently reminded me that it was good manners to cover our mouths when we yawned.

"Ma'am, buy bananas for the child!"

A man carrying a basket full of bananas peered through my window, as if to discern my exact age. I stretched my arms sideways to relieve my tense muscles, then placed the back of my hand behind my neck to protect it from the hot red vinyl. I could feel drops of sweat trickling down the sides of my face. Using my free hand, I wiped the sweat off my face in one swift motion. Aunt Agnes ignored the man with the bananas and instead looked back to where I was sitting.

"Are you too warm?"

I shook my head, afraid to disclose any discomfort I could have been experiencing in case I should offend her. Aunt Agnes' presence was paralyzing. When she spoke, my tongue froze and I struggled to find words to make any intelligent response. If only I could get out of the car and escape from her. I fidgeted in my seat, countless questions running through my mind, yet unable to express any of them. Why could I not be with my brother and sisters? I didn't understand why I was going to live with this particular aunt, whom I hardly knew. If she had been that close to Mama, I could not understand why I had never seen her at our house. Uncle Eliud used to visit us, and in my understanding, that meant he loved us. Aunt Agnes' absence from our lives prior to Mama's death made me wonder if she really liked our family.

"Are you hungry?" Aunt Agnes asked. My stomach rumbled, and I suddenly became aware of intense hunger pangs. I could have eaten anything. But it was so much easier to lie than to admit to her that I might need her maternal intervention. And so, again I shook my head. I was beginning to notice her detached manner of speaking to me, and I could not bring myself to trust her. Most importantly, I wasn't about to let her think I accepted being separated from my family. Wasn't it enough that I was hurt by the fact that no one had even attempted to explain to me what was happening and why we were being sent off to different homes, and for how long? Unable to control anything that had happened around me in the last few days, I held on to what I could. I was not going to let her, or anyone else, replace Mama.

There was a moment of awkward silence as she stared at me. I fidgeted again, unable to think of what to say. I looked out the window to see if the street vendors were still nearby. The man with the bananas was trying to sell his produce to another traveler nearby. I swallowed hard as I thought about how sweet the bananas would be. A child sitting on a small blanket peeled a fat yellow banana and took a generous bite. If my mouth had been open, I could have drooled. Instead, I swallowed again. I watched the banana disappear quickly while the child chewed hungrily and began to contemplate giving in to my famished state.

"We are going to Nairobi," Aunt Agnes said, interrupting my battling mind. The subject had now changed, and I had lost my opportunity to eat.

"Nairobi is a very big city," she continued with feigned gentleness. Was she trying to win my affection?

I raised my eyes to look into hers, feeling conflicted between a deep desire to connect with her and respond to the friendliness she was displaying, and a strong will to defend the little dignity I had left. I looked at her, unable to say anything.

"You will like it there," she said as her cheeks gave way to a smile.

I forced a half smile, longing for David and my sisters. Fresh memories of our trip to Nairobi earlier that month came pouring into my mind. On that trip I had stayed awake, not wanting to miss any of the changing landscape during the four-hour journey. David and I had screamed in excitement as we passed herds of zebras and giraffes along the way. But this time I was not interested in looking at anything. Sadness gripped my heart as I struggled to retain glimpses of those precious memories that were threatening to slip away to join Mama, forever gone from me. Afraid that Aunt Agnes might notice how sad I was and think I didn't appreciate what she was doing for me, I forced myself to be in the present.

Uncle Gideon came back to the car and, soon after, we were on our way again. The rest of the journey was quiet. Aunt Agnes fell asleep and I stayed awake and stared out the window in blank dismay. Two hours later, we arrived at our destination.

The car pulled up outside an alley between rows of two storied buildings. I had never seen so many identical houses arranged so neatly in one confined location. We stopped right outside a building where several children were playing in the alley. I strained my neck to see how many there were.

"Margy, your mom is back! Margy, your mom is back!" A girl called out in a tone that sounded like she was warning someone.

"Margy," I repeated the name quietly, remembering my sister Margy. Just then, another girl about my age came running from behind the building where we had stopped. She glanced toward the car as if to confirm the warning. As soon as she saw us, she quickly dropped a ball she was holding, sped past the car toward the building, then up the flight of stairs, made a right and ran through a door with number 9D written on it.

"Margy is in trouble! Margy is in trouble!" another child shouted repeatedly.

Aunt Agnes and Uncle Gideon got out of the car. I waited for instructions as my instincts told me to behave myself around them. Aunt Agnes opened the car door on my side. As I stepped out of the car, I couldn't help wondering why Margy would be in trouble. I used to be very excited whenever Mama came back home. I would run to meet her, and she always scooped me in her arms. This would be followed by asking what she had brought for me. I could not remember any incident where any of us would have been in fear when she came home. Even when I'd been naughty, it was never the first thing Mama dealt with upon arrival.

As Aunt Agnes led the way, I followed her up the stairs, entered the house, and proceeded to the living room as she directed. The house was a little smaller than our home in Eldoret. On my way in, I had noticed a closed door on the left, which I later discovered was the master bedroom. This had been followed by a narrow short corridor with a kitchen on the left and a small shower stall on the right. Next to the shower stall was a toilet. There was a door separating the corridor and the small living room, where I now waited for further instructions before I could proceed.

"Go ahead, take a seat," Uncle Gideon said in a somewhat stern voice, startling me. His voice sounded firmer than I had imagined it would be. He had not said anything to me since we had left Eldoret, and I had secretly hoped he would sound like Uncle Eliud. Disappointed that he might not be like the uncle I loved, I simply obeyed and took the closest seat I could find—the sofa. Uncle Gideon walked past me with my suitcase in his hand, carrying it to a second bedroom, apparently Margy's. As soon as he opened the door, I heard someone quickly jump to a bed. The sound was familiar and it reminded me of how I had often playfully jumped onto Mama's bed. I looked through the open door to see who it was. There were two single beds, one on each side of the room, and sitting on one of the beds was Margy.

"Margy, come and meet you new sister Susie," Uncle Gideon said as he placed my suitcase in the middle of the bedroom floor. *New sister?*

Margy walked shyly toward me and slowly stretched her hand to shake mine. I took her hand to return her greeting. To my surprise, a second girl came from that same bedroom to greet me.

"This is Ramona," Uncle Gideon said without offering an explanation. I later found out that Ramona was the maid. This was a new concept for me, since Mama had never had a maid.

"Ramona, make us some tea," Aunt Agnes instructed as she made her way to the living room. Ramona quickly reappeared from the bedroom and marched to the kitchen. Margy followed quickly and closed the living room door behind them. Aunt Agnes then sat next to me. I tensed up and moved slightly away from her. I was having a hard time relaxing in her presence, and her closeness sent a strange chill down my spine.

"This is now your new home," she explained. "You are to call me Mama and this is Papa." Uncle Gideon, who had taken a seat across the room, looked in my direction in confirmation.

I nodded in response, unsure of how to interpret what I was hearing. It was becoming obvious that my identity was changing. Losing Mama was traumatic enough for me, and to add these changes to my family structure was more than I could bear. I needed some real explanation, someone to tell me what all these changes meant. Was I ever going to see my family again? I still wasn't willing to allow anyone to replace Mama. In my defiant need to control some aspects of all that was changing so quickly, I determined to address Aunt Agnes and Uncle Gideon in a formal style, so they became Mother and Father.

"Margy is now your sister and you must, therefore, forget about your family. Do you understand?" Mother's words dropped like a bombshell. I was still adjusting to thinking of them as Mother and Father. To be told so bluntly that I was to forget my family hit me like a rock between my eyes. My heart flipped and my body began to shake. I looked at Father, hoping he would intervene. His face was buried in a newspaper, and I wasn't even sure he'd heard what she had just said.

"You will be the first-born and Margy the second born," Mother continued. I looked at her unbelievingly. She seemed oblivious to my emotions.

"You must also remember that we are doing you a favor by taking you in, since no one else could take you. You must, therefore, always be thankful and do all we ask of you. Do you understand?"

My body was shaking so violently I was certain she could feel the sofa shake. Feelings of rejection set in as I pondered what I had just heard. No one wanted me!

The words echoed in my head over and over. The feeling of being hit by a brick ran from the middle of my forehead down to my abdomen, making me aware of a sudden need to relieve myself. I was also very hungry and thirsty. Deciding the toilet was my highest priority, I turned toward Mother and asked her as politely as I could, "May I please use the toilet?"

Without waiting for her approval, I ran toward the door I had noticed across from the kitchen. As soon as I closed the bathroom door behind me, I began to sob violently, but was careful not to be heard. I couldn't trust anyone with my pain. I longed for Mama. She was much gentler with me. Several minutes went by before I finally stopped crying. I wiped my face with the toilet paper and used the toilet. The thought of going back to the living room frightened me. I couldn't imagine what was in store. It had been a long day and all I longed for was just some time to myself to think through all that was happening. But I was afraid of Mother. Not wanting to aggravate her, I decided it was best not to delay any longer. As I passed by the kitchen, I wished I could join Margy and Ramona, but I didn't dare. As I resumed my seat on the sofa next to Mother, I stuck my fingers in my mouth.

"What are you doing?" Mother yelled as she roughly pulled my fingers out of my mouth.

"I'm sorry," I said, shocked by her reaction. Even though Mama had often encouraged me to stop this habit, she had never been that forceful. Unable to control my emotions in Mother's presence any longer, I buried my head on my lap and broke down in painful sobs.

"You must never put those fingers in your mouth again, do you understand?" I heard Mother yell. I could not believe how unsympathetic she seemed to be. As she screamed at me, I became increasingly afraid of her to the point that this fear became greater than the ripping of my heart that was causing me to cry. All the things that meant the world to me were mercilessly being torn away. It was this fear that caused me to stop crying just as Ramona walked in with a tray of tea.

As I sipped on the tea, I realized that it didn't taste anything like the tea Mama used to make. I couldn't decide whether it was the salty taste in my mouth from all the crying that caused the strange flavor, or if things were just going to be that different in this home. In the few hours I'd spent with Mother and Father, it was clear that they were not as kind as Mama had been, and when they spoke they sounded angry, which made me scared. Margy and Ramona's anxious faces only served as proof that life here was going to be an unwelcome shock to my system.

Chapter 6
Margy and I

From left: Margy, Ramona and Susie

He Really Is My Father

The first supper at my new home lasted a long time, as I labored through mouthfuls of hardened cornmeal mush and overcooked cabbage. I dared not complain, aware that I was fortunate to have been taken in by this family. As Margy later showed me my assigned bed, I was relieved to be away from Mother and Father's presence. Margy, whom I preferred to think of as a cousin rather than a sister, slept on the other bed. Ramona pulled some bedding from underneath Margy's bed and, to my amazement, laid it on the floor and crawled under the blankets. I could not believe this—I had never seen anyone sleep on the floor without a mattress.

"Why do you have to sleep on the floor like that?" I asked.

"Because she is the maid," Margy answered.

"You can sleep with me," I offered.

"She will be in trouble if she does."

"I will say I told her she could."

"Thanks, but I can't," Ramona said sadly.

Unable to convince her, I proceeded to prepare for bed. I bent down to open my suitcase, still on the floor where Father had placed it earlier. As I shoved clothes aside in search of my nightdress, Margy's mouth dropped. She looked at me in obvious wonderment. Surprised by how impressed she seemed to be, I offered to give her some of my clothes. For a moment I even forgot my own sadness, looking at Margy whose mouth was still open. I browsed through the suitcase to see what I could give her. Each of my dresses represented a fond memory of moments shared with Mama, as she had always helped me get dressed. I was not ready to let go of this special link to her. For this reason, sharing the clothes seemed better than giving, so I told Margy she could wear anything she wanted.

"You can be my sister if you like," I added, wanting to offer her some of the happiness I had known growing up with my family. I had resented the idea of calling her sister when Father had first brought it up, but now, seeing how unhappy she seemed to be, treating her like a sister wasn't too much to give to her. As I slipped into my nightdress, I noticed she wasn't wearing anything except her underwear.

"Don't you have a nightdress?"

She shook her head. I reached back in my suitcase to find a spare one, but just as I was handing it to her, Ramona informed me that Margy was not allowed to sleep in any clothes.

"Why?" I asked, not having ever known anyone who didn't sleep with night clothes.

"She wets her bed."

Margy retreated into her bed in embarrassment. I got into my own bed and pulled the blankets over my body. The letters MOD were printed on the top blanket. I raised my head to look at the bottom one to see if there was anything printed on it. The same letters were there too. Ramona's and Margy's blankets had the same letters printed on them.

"What is MOD?"

"Ministry of Defense," Margy responded proudly, relieved that the subject of bed-wetting had been changed. That night I learned that this house was on the Kenya Air Force base, which explained the military-style order I had observed when we had arrived. Father was a sergeant by rank and worked as an aircraft technician. Mother, on the other hand, was a nurse.

The following morning, I awoke to Father's stern voice as he pulled my blankets off my bed, commanding me to get up. His disapproving look at the fingers in my mouth reminded me I had been ordered to stop this habit.

After showering, I went to the kitchen where Ramona was busy washing breakfast dishes. Margy had gone to school. As Ramona served me breakfast, I took the opportunity to learn as much as possible about the family. As she spoke in her kind, non-threatening tenderness, I found out that Margy was not Mother and Father's child either. At the age of sixteen, Father's sister had given birth to Margy. Father's sister had been too young and needed to continue with school, so Mother and Father, who were childless, had taken Margy. Margy had only been six months old at the time, so they were the only parents she'd ever known. Margy's mother had never had anything more to do with Margy and, as a result, Margy did not know anything about her background. I didn't know of any other children who were being raised by people other than their parents, so I wondered whether it was typical for such children not to receive the kind of love and care I had enjoyed with Mama. The facts about Margy gave me a sense of kinship with her.

"Susie!" Father called impatiently from the living room, interrupting my conversation with Ramona. He informed me that I would be enrolling in Margy's school. We got into the car and drove in silence to where I would be starting my new school. As we talked with the headmaster at Eastleigh Airport Primary School later that morning, I was shocked to learn that my name was now Susie Keiyu. When Mother had informed me that they would be my parents, it never occurred to me that I would also be receiving a new last name. There didn't seem to be an end to ways in which my identity was changing. And so, as Margy and I started attending the same school, I became known as Margy's big sister.

Chapter 7

Enduring

Gazing out the window one afternoon, I watched children playing in mud puddles just outside our house. It had been raining heavily all day, and Mother and Father were at home. We stayed in our bedroom, trying to entertain ourselves, waiting to be told when to work on the next chore. It had not taken long before I was expected to join Margy and Ramona in assuming household responsibilities. And with them came punishment when we didn't live up to the expected standards. This came in the form of beatings—different from any I had ever experienced. Thinking improved behavior could cause them to like me, I worked hard to win the affection of Mother and Father. If it really was true that no one else wanted me, I hoped that, if I did my best,

I could at least win their approval and then it wouldn't matter that I was not wanted.

When washing clothes I made sure the collars were thoroughly scrubbed, as they seemed to need extra attention. Mother always inspected that particular area to see if the brown discoloration from sweat mixed with hair grease had come off. Father seemed more concerned about shoes being polished to a perfect shine, so you could almost see your reflection as in a mirror. Dishes had to be washed after each meal, regardless of how late dinner had been served. One late night, Margy and I were arguing about who would wash the dishes and who would dry them. We both preferred drying, so we reached for the dishcloth at the same time. As we tried to each take it away from the other, Margy accidentally slipped and her body hit the edge of the kitchen counter, causing the heap of dirty dishes to crash on the floor.

"What is going on?" Mother yelled from the living room.

We quickly reached down to pick up the mess before anyone could see the damage. Father came to investigate. He walked into the kitchen just as Margy was getting back on her feet. One look at Father was enough to tell me we were in for a serious beating. He commanded the three of us to lie on the floor, where we always found ourselves when being disciplined. From the corner of my eye, I saw Father take off his belt, which meant that he was too angry to go find the electric cord kept especially for this purpose. The punishment methods varied. Depending on how mad he was, sometimes he used any object he could lay his hands on. If not his belt, he might use a wooden spoon or the back of his hand to hit us. The electric cord used on good days was about half an inch wide and two feet long. Whatever the weapon, he would beat us mercilessly until he was exhausted. After the beating, we were required to thank him for the punishment, to show we appreciated the fact that he was training us to be good kids.

Wham!

I heard the first stroke hit Margy, who was lying on my right. This was followed by a scream as she cried out in agony. I flinched in pain as the belt hit my back. The next stroke followed, hitting me slightly below my tiny bottom, stiff with fear. I started sobbing softly, afraid to provoke him further if I cried out loud. Margy wiggled on the floor in pain as the strokes continued to rain on the three of us. Her wiggling and crying must have evoked more anger, because the strokes became more rapid and harder, randomly hitting us all over our bodies. One hit me at the back of my neck with such severity that I let out a shrieking sound and jerked forward. Thinking I was trying to escape, he pegged me down with his foot on the small of my back to hold me in place, then struck me repeatedly to punish me for my attempted getaway. Closing my eyes tightly, hoping to block out the pain, I cried in silent desperation. Father removed his foot from my back and resumed beating us, Ramona included by proximity. Ramona always endured her pain quietly. I felt terrible because she didn't deserve to be part of this punishment. But I, too, had often been whipped for crimes I had no part in. The policy seemed to be "guilty by association."

When he was done, he simply put his belt back on and ordered us to get up. Like obedient animals, we got on our feet and thanked him, bowing toward him as was required.

Household chores were not the only areas that caused problems at home. Margy struggled with school. She had a hard time spelling, and couldn't do math. Reading was also difficult for her. Both Mother and Father constantly tormented her, often calling her stupid. Father was particularly harsh. He would hit her on the head or hurt her in other ways if she couldn't answer questions relating to her homework. I felt sorry for her and helped her whenever I could. But this became increasingly difficult because Father would sit in the same room with us to be sure we were doing our work. One night, Mother sat on the sofa knitting while Margy and I struggled through a class project. Father came to see what we were doing.

"What are you working on?" he asked Margy.

"Math."

"Let me see," he said as he pulled her book to take a closer look. She was in the middle of solving a problem.

Knowing that it would likely lead to trouble if Margy failed to answer Father's question correctly, I nervously fidgeted in my seat.

"What is thirty-three divided by eleven?"

Margy did not respond. He asked again, more impatiently this time. I squirmed, wishing I could find a way to write three without being seen, but Father was too close and I didn't want to get into trouble. Tears started rolling down Margy's face.

"How can you be so stupid?" Father asked as Margy twitched. He was pinching her ear, a tactic he used to get her to speak.

"Maybe Susie can tell you," he said looking at me. I hated this, because I knew it made Margy more uncomfortable when she was compared with me.

"Three," I said, praying he would leave her alone.

"See how easy it is?" he mocked. I looked down, feeling sorry that by answering I had made Margy look stupid.

"What is fifty-five divided by eleven?"

Margy sobbed softly. Father took one of Mother's knitting needles and brought it to the table.

"If you don't answer, I will stick this in your nose."

I hoped he was teasing, but he wasn't. He inserted the needle in one of her nostrils and slowly pushed.

"This feels good, doesn't it?" He taunted as he pushed the needle further into her nostril. Margy looked into his eyes, begging for mercy. I started to cry too. Margy tried to move away from him, but he held her down and continued to push the needle. Her tears turned into loud sobs. This infuriated him and he slapped her across the face. The unexpected force pushed her toward me. I threw my arms around her protectively. I held my breath, expecting to be hit. To my relief, Father cursed out loud and left the room. That night I began to hate him.

After school, we made the most of our time alone at home before Mother and Father came back from work. Being outdoors was against the rules, so as we played with friends, we kept careful track of time so we wouldn't be caught outside. In the evenings and on weekends, we would become the quiet, compliant kids that Mother and Father had trained us to be. One Sunday afternoon, as we sat quietly, taking a short rest before the evening chores started, a change occurred that would further define our status.

"Throw the ball!" A young boy shouted as we watched the children playing in the alley in front of our house. A ball had come bouncing onto our veranda. Margy took it and threw it back to the boy. The boy fell on top of another child as they raced for the ball, causing Margy to burst into uninhibited laughter.

"Hush!" I whispered, aware that Mother, who was taking a nap in the bedroom with the window facing the veranda, usually listened to be sure we weren't playing.

Ramona came out to the veranda, carrying a small bag. She seemed a little tense, but I didn't think it was unusual, because we all felt tense most of the time. She was wearing the same dress she had worn when we had gone to church that morning. This was one of three outfits she owned. She glanced at Margy and me, and then slowly walked down the steps. I looked at Margy and we both shrugged, wondering where she was going. As she walked toward the gates, we assumed Mother had asked her to go to the market just outside the base.

An hour later, Mother called for us to begin the evening chores. Margy started chopping collard greens while I ironed our clothes.

"Where is Ramona?" Mother asked.

Confused, I quickly glanced at her and then proceeded with ironing. She went to the kitchen and asked Margy, who, like me, did not answer. Mother went to our bedroom and then outside to search for Ramona. We followed her curiously.

"Have you seen Ramona?" we heard her ask a neighbor.

"I saw her going that way," the neighbor responded pointing toward the road.

Mother went back to our bedroom and searched through the box where Ramona kept her clothes. They were missing. Margy and I looked at each other, suddenly understanding what was happening. Ramona had run away. From the look in Mother's eyes, we knew she had come to the same conclusion. She then stormed into her bedroom, angrily slamming the door behind her. The matter was never discussed.

Since there was no longer a maid, Margy and I slipped into the role of taking care of all the chores, even cooking. We were hardly tall enough to reach the electric stove and had to use a small stepstool so we could cook. Our daily chores were extended to include work on the three section farms Mother and Father owned. The Air Force administration had allocated land to all the residents for subsistence farming. This land was subdivided into small sections, so anyone interested could take as many as desired. Ours were located on the south side of our house, in clear view of our front door, which meant that Mother could keep a watchful eye on us when we were working.

Mother preferred that all the harvested crops be kept in our tiny bedroom to ensure safekeeping. Sacks of unhusked maize and beans piled up between our beds, leaving just enough room for us to squeeze through. Husking filled the room with dust that would cause us to cough for days. After husking we used our hands to separate the dried kernels of corn from the cob. This process caused painful blisters that made working with our hands more difficult.

Unprocessed dry beans still in the pods would also cause small cuts all over our skin as we walked passed them, making us scratch uncontrollably, so that our bodies would end up with sores that hurt when we showered. To separate the beans from the pods, we used a broomstick to hit the sacks, after which we would pull out the empty pods and dry leaves. Using two baskets, we would then pour the beans from one basket to the other, allowing the wind to blow off the chaff.

Our nighttime routine was also changing. Mother, who often complained of high blood pressure, required special attention. Each night after the supper dishes were cleaned and put away, we would bring her a glass of water to drink with her medication. Then we would wash her feet in warm water and wipe them with a towel. We would also massage her scalp with oil before braiding her hair for the night. Hard as our young lives seemed to be, I started looking forward to this nightly ritual, because it made us feel connected to her. Though longing to be close, we still never seemed to please either her or Father. To them, we were nothing more than little maids.

The more we seemed to fail to live up to Mother and Father's expectations, the harder I tried to please them. Over and over I drew attention to what I seemed to do best, my academics. Mama's death had not affected my ability to do well in school. I tried each term to highlight this success, hoping that somehow Mother and Father would praise me.

"I did it again! I did it again!" I yelled in excitement one evening as I waved my report card toward Mother. I had ranked fifth in my class. The teacher had commented on my good work when she handed me the report card earlier that morning. The afternoon had been a long wait, as I eagerly anticipated sharing the joy with Mother and Father when they came home from work. Mother was the first to arrive, and as soon as she walked through the door, I picked the report card from the table where I had kept a protective eye on it all afternoon.

"Let's see," she said taking it from my hands. She glanced at it and gave it back to me without saying anything.

"What do you think?" I asked.

"Only fools are excited about being fifth."

Wounded, I watched as she walked to her bedroom to change from her nurse's uniform. I felt rejected. I longed for kindness from her, even just a pat on my shoulder or some encouraging words; something to help me feel like I meant something to her. Instead, all she left behind as she walked away from me was the hospital smell that I had come to associate with her arrival. As Mother disappeared into the bedroom after ignoring my success that evening, I felt the emotional distance between us increase. Hard as I tried, I couldn't seem to close this gap. I went to our bedroom and stared out the window to pass the time. Would anyone ever want me?

Term after term, I looked forward to my report card, hoping that as teachers praised me, it would become obvious at home that I was good at something. Even my classmates held me in high esteem. But one day, the attention I received was of a very different nature. During my fifth year of primary school, a boy named Karume took an interest in me. I didn't know anything about boys, except that Mother and Father continually told us never to talk to them, with the threat that if we ever became pregnant, we would be sent away.

The day had been going on as usual, but since we had a free period, the kids were rowdy. Everyone took advantage of the absence of a teacher in the room. Then I noticed a piece of paper being passed from Karume and headed in my direction. One naughty boy took the liberty to open it. He then read it out loud: Susie, I love you. Karume. The class burst into roaring laughter. Embarrassed, I placed my head on my desk and covered it with my hands, wishing I could disappear. This was not the kind of attention I longed for.

In the two years that followed, I worked hard at ignoring Karume and boys in general. At the end of my seventh grade, I sat for the Certificate of Primary Education (CPE) national exams. Passing them guaranteed entry into form one, the beginning of secondary school. Mother actually prayed for me on the morning of the exams. I was very surprised at the gesture, but cherished the moment and hoped that her prayers would be answered. The results wouldn't be out till the beginning of the year, so we had to wait at least two months.

In the meantime Christmas came, and we would be reminded of just how bad we had been, and why we didn't deserve any gifts. Mother always kept score of our wrongs and, no matter how hard we tried, whatever "good" we did was never enough. The Air Force organized a children's party each year where all the children and their parents went to celebrate with Father Christmas. It was a very special event marked by games like tug-of-war and soccer. The highlight of the party, however, was when Father Christmas arrived in a helicopter, carrying a large gift box. As soon as he landed, a rope would be tied around his waist and all the children would pull him, bringing him to a stage with a large Christmas tree decorated with ornaments and cotton wool. For once, this year we were allowed to attend.

Both Mother and Father participated in the parents' activities. It was really nice to see them laugh. In the midst of all this, though, I couldn't wait for the special time when the gifts would be distributed. It would be the first time in four years that I would receive a present. The last time had been a year after Mama's death, when Margreet and Wim Bouw had come to say goodbye. Their term as missionaries in Kenya was over and they were going back to Holland. They had given me a plastic tea set, while Margy had received a doll. Soon after they left, Mother came into our room and asked for the gifts, saying we didn't deserve them.

I had gone to my room and knelt on my bed to look out the window, as I often did whenever I felt sad. Remembering what Mother and Father always said about our being undeserving of all we received from them, I felt unworthy. The words Mother had said to me when I first arrived echoed in my head. She had told me that no one wanted me, which, over the years, had translated to my being unworthy. As I continually failed in their eyes, those words ran through my mind like a continuous tape, leaving me feeling guilty and unable to enjoy anything. I was afraid that everything, including the home I lived in, could be taken away, just as Mama had been taken away from me.

There had been another time when an uncle brought us beautiful blouses from a trip he'd made to Israel, and dresses from a later trip to the UK. Each of these times, Mother had taken the clothes away, claiming they were too good for us. We wondered what she did with some of our gifts that seemed only appropriate for children.

As we now waited for the presents from Father Christmas, I wondered if things would be different this time. When my name was called, I walked up to the stage beaming. Regardless of what happened to the gifts later, I was determined to enjoy this moment. Neighbors were going to see me participate in what other kids deemed normal. I felt like everyone else for a change. My heart raced in anticipation as Father Christmas handed me a nicely wrapped package. Receiving a present was such a rare experience for me. I went back to my seat and waited for Margy to receive hers, to see what she would do. When she came back, we both looked at Mother, who was sitting next to us, wondering if she would allow us to open them. From the look in her eyes, we knew she preferred we didn't open them just yet. We waited impatiently as others ripped theirs open, exuberance all over their faces. When the party was over, the four of us walked home, Margy and I in silence, while Mother and Father talked to each other. Once at home, with Mother's permission, we quickly tore the presents open, anxious to see what we had received. Mine was an expensive-looking pen set. It seemed appropriate, since I would be starting a new school at the beginning of the year. I was really excited and imagined myself showing it off to my new friends. Margy's was a box of assorted imported chocolates. But the joy of receiving presents was short lived because, as always, Mother took the gifts away, reinforcing my sense of unworthiness. By the time January came and my CPE results were out, I had no desire to even try to seek praise, so even though Mother's prayers were answered and I had passed with flying colors, it was with great reservation that I gave her the news. I was accepted at Moi Forces Academy (MFA), a new prestigious school built specifically for military children. But even such an accomplishment did not change how I was treated at home.

The first Sunday after having starting school at MFA, Margy and I sat outside after lunch while Mother settled for her usual Sunday afternoon nap. Father had gone to the mess for a drink. When he came back later, we acknowledged his return and continued to sit outside, since it was still early and we didn't need to start with our Sunday chores yet. Our quiet afternoon was suddenly interrupted by what sounded like an argument between Mother and Father. They never got into arguments so, believing it may have had something to do with us, we were alarmed. After several minutes, Mother came out to where we were.

"Margy, why didn't you take your beddings out today?" she asked in an irritated voice.

Margy, who still struggled with her bed-wetting problem, was required to hang her wet blankets on the clothesline outside every day, and to wash them on Saturdays. Her problem meant that our bedroom had a permanent urine smell, and the stench usually worsened if she forgot to take the blankets out to dry.

Margy silently rose and proceeded to correct her mistake. It wasn't the first time she had needed a reminder, so I didn't think anything of it. By the time she came back, both Mother and Father were talking at the same time telling us how irresponsible and ungrateful we were—the usual. But this time, for punishment, Father decided he would shave our heads. Thinking he was joking, I rose to my feet and looked at him. He already had a pair of scissors and a towel.

"Go bring a stool!" he ordered Margy who was standing closest to him.

Obediently, she ran to the house and brought the stool. Father began to shave her head as I watched in utter shock. I was next. All I could think of was my new school and how humiliating it would be to show up the next day with a shaved head. I was angry, but powerless. I could not believe that Mother, who most likely understood the importance of hair for girls, wasn't even attempting to stop him. Halfway through the process a neighbor, the chaplain of the Air Force base Anglican Church, stopped by. He tried to intervene, but Father maintained that we did not need hair. He worked diligently, making sure none of it was left on my head. When he finished, he ordered me to go and clean myself. I walked to the house feeling disappointed that the chaplain had shown up too late. As I sat quietly at supper that night, picking at my food without any appetite, I prayed for a miracle. There was no miracle, and Monday came far too soon.

Chapter 8

My Conversion

Being humiliated at such an early stage in the new school didn't make me the most popular kid. The Christian Union was the only non-threatening club I could participate in. I longed to be somewhere that gave me some significance. If God cared, then hopefully, people associated with godly things might care. The Youth for Christ team that led the meetings seemed nice and affirmed all who came.

Margy and I went to church every Sunday, but according to Mother, our behavior guaranteed a place in hell. She often talked about our need to become saved, saying that this was the only way we could go to heaven, but she had never explained just how we could be saved. At the Christian Union I felt accepted, but I still needed to become that child who could make Mother and

Father happy. So, one afternoon, as I listened to the Youth for Christ representative share the story of Nicodemus, and how he had asked Jesus about being born again, I paid careful attention. I was fascinated by the non-condescending manner in which Jesus had responded to Nicodemus when he had asked the question about being born again. Then I heard about how God so loved the world that he gave his only Son. If we believed in Him we would have life, and I wanted to be part of that. For six years I had experienced so little love that I wanted to just soak in this abundance of love I was hearing about. Could it be true that God could love me so completely and unconditionally?

The speaker continued to explain that to receive God's forgiveness, I would need to acknowledge that I was a sinner and unable to save myself. By accepting Jesus the Son of God into my heart and allowing him to be the Lord of my life, I would have eternal life and acceptance into God's kingdom. How I needed acceptance! I knew I was a sinner; Mother had constantly reminded me of that. Oh, how wonderful it would be to tell her I was finally clean! Perhaps this was the magic that would earn me the closeness I longed for at home. I would become the perfect child!

I was the first to walk forward when the invitation to receive Jesus was made. Those of us who had responded to this call were to repeat a simple prayer as led by the speaker. With tears running down my face, I confessed

My Conversion

my sins, acknowledging that Mother and Father had warned me about my inability to be good. I was now ready to leave my sinful life behind and start a new life. When I repeated the part about asking Jesus to come into my heart, I felt as though something physical took place in my body. An overwhelming sense of being cleansed came and just lifted a heavy load off my shoulder. I knew instantly that something had changed, and couldn't wait to get home and tell Mother. She would finally have the child she always wanted.

At the opportune time, as I stood in the kitchen watching Mother clean around the sink area, I spoke.

"Mother, today I asked Jesus to come into my heart and now I am born again." The speaker at the meeting had encouraged me to share this news with others. Not that I needed the encouragement. This was a life changing event, and the sooner I let Mother know, the better life was going to become. She had waited so long for me to become the person she could unreservedly pour out her love to. There was no wasting time. I waited for a hug, an embrace. Would she dance with joy, saying that at last her prayers had been answered? The seconds ticked by. I turned around to face her in anticipation. And then, finally, one simple word came out of her mouth.

"You?" She laughed sarcastically, as though I had made the most outrageous remark about myself. Dropping the washcloth into the sink, she continued her degrading speech. "There's no way a person like you can be saved." She spoke with conviction, sounding more agitated now as she hung the washcloth on the faucet to dry.

I stared at her in disbelief, shocked by what I had just heard. *Of course, she is right. How could I forget that I am such a terrible person?* For a long time, something inside me had been slowly dying. The power of demeaning words spoken to us countless times over the last six years had been gradually killing any glimmer of hope that I was lovable. Even more than the beatings we received, I dreaded the hurtful words that Mother and Father unleashed upon us. These words often pierced through the heart so deeply, cutting through the very core of our being and transforming us into all they said we were: unworthy.

This sense of unworthiness is what I had noticed in Margy's demeanor when I first came. I was beginning to think of myself in the same way. Bruises from the beatings healed, but the wounds from their words festered endlessly, piling up on top of one another to reinforce the intended message. The message of those words left me no choice but to become what Mother and Father said I was. Even at night when I lay down to sleep, I could hear their voices echoing through my ears, like a tape with an endless loop, reminding me of my inadequacy and hopelessness, a tape I could not turn off once it started playing. Moments earlier, I had been eager to share my newfound faith. I had hoped that, finally, I would amount to something. And now, in a split second, the little light of hope that had begun to shine had been snuffed out, and I had returned to despair. I was not even good enough for God.

Chapter 9

Coup d'Etat

The following year, it became mandatory to board at my school, a welcome option for me that provided a temporary escape from life at home. I was fourteen. Lydia and my other sisters had recently come back into my life. Having been ordered to forget about them, I hardly knew how to address them. We had been separated for so long, I didn't know how they felt about me, or where they stood in relation to Mother's decision that I forget about them. They were like strangers to me. Lydia, in an attempt to re-establish our relationship, came to visit me at school. It was just before August of 1982. To my surprise, she handed me a package.

"What have you brought me?" I asked, unaccustomed to receiving any gifts.

"Why don't you see for yourself?"

He Really Is My Father

I quickly tore open the gift box, exposing a beautiful bright pink dress. It was the most beautiful dress I had ever owned, and I couldn't wait to show it to my roommates, and to wear it to church on the Sunday after we returned home for the upcoming holidays.

I hugged her just as I had seen other kids do whenever they were visited by loved ones. It felt strange, as it was such a new experience for me.

"I also have something to tell you," Lydia said as she released me from the hug. "I am getting married!"

I was stunned. There had been nothing to prepare me for such news. Mother and Father had told us that boys were bad. Two years earlier, Mother had announced that Judy and Margy had had babies. It had been a scandal for Mother, because they were unmarried. But since I hardly knew them, it had not affected me significantly. I had not even seen the children. Lydia's upcoming marriage was threatening, because I was hoping to have a relationship with her. I needed a big sister. I had been forced into a firstborn role at Mother's, and now I was ready to go back to being the baby I once was. If Lydia were to get married, would this ever be possible? Would there ever be room for me in her life?

I looked at her suspiciously, wondering if she, too, was pregnant. No one had ever talked to me about boyfriends in a way to help me understand their role in preparing for marriage. All I knew was that boys made girls pregnant, and that was a very bad thing.

Coup d'Etat

"Aren't you happy for me?" Lydia asked quizzically.

I bowed my head in embarrassment. I just had no ability to express any emotions, good or bad. At Mother's, your thoughts didn't count. You just accepted life as it came. You had no say in anything. Because of this, Lydia's question sounded rhetorical. And so, it was with resigned acceptance to the new reality that I bid her farewell when it was time for her to go.

My first Saturday home from school, Lydia was to bring her fiancé Peter to meet our family for the first time. Mother prepared a special meal for them, explaining that Margy and I weren't skilled enough to cook for such occasions. Lydia and Peter arrived just in time to enjoy the carefully prepared rice and curry dish. I still didn't know what to think about the engagement and felt confused by the fact that Mother, who had been so opposed to the idea of boyfriends, was actually celebrating Lydia's relationship. Perhaps it was OK as long as the relationship was kept a secret. That seemed to be a logical explanation, as I couldn't imagine how Mother would have agreed to Lydia having a boyfriend. And then, there would have to be no pregnancy. As I watched Lydia and Peter being treated very well, I gave myself permission to have a boyfriend someday, as long as I kept it secret.

Later that night, before going to bed I laid out the dress that Lydia had bought me in preparation for Sunday. Margy and I talked long into the night before falling asleep, since it was only my second day home from boarding school. At around 3:00 a.m. I was awakened by the sound of gunshots. They sounded close. I sat up in my bed to listen, just to be sure I wasn't dreaming.

Bang! Bang! Bang! The sound came again, and I quickly pulled the covers over my head as if the gun shots were coming right through the window.

"Margy! Margy!" I called from under my blankets.

"What?" she responded sleepily.

"Did you hear that?"

"Hear what?"

"The gunshots."

Bang! Bang! Bang! The sound came again, causing Margy to pull her blankets over her head. A few seconds later she knelt on her bed and peeked through the corner of the curtain to see if there was anything visible.

"It sounds like practice," she said going back to bed.

Coup d'Etat

The sounds continued through the night as we peeked between gunshots to see if we could see the source. We had never experienced a war. Although Kenya was considered a peaceful country, judging from what we had seen on television about wars in countries like neighboring Uganda, we were afraid that something similar could be happening to us. We knew that Father would be involved in a war because of his job as a soldier, and we feared for his life. We also worried about the effect on us as residents at the Air Force base. After talking about the different possibilities, we decided to try and sleep, hoping that by morning things would be clearer.

At 7:00 a.m. Mother came to our bedroom, quietly opening the door. I peeked through the blankets I'd pulled over my head.

"Shhh," she hushed, as she walked closer to where I was sleeping.

"You must be very quiet," she continued. "There's been a coup and the government has been overthrown." She then explained that Father had to report to work, and we would know more when he returned. She told us that we had to stay in the house until further notice.

"Wow! Can you believe that?" I asked as I threw the blankets off. I couldn't sleep anymore. This was exciting and scary at the same time. There was a sense of adventure to our otherwise boring life. But at the same time, we were aware that other countries that had experienced coups sometimes ended up having civil wars, and innocent civilians died. As I paced up and down in the room, talking excitedly about what was happening, I noticed the pink dress I had carefully laid out in anticipation for church.

"I guess I won't be wearing this today," I said with disappointment as I took the dress and began to fold it.

We later learned that the coup had been started by some low ranking Air Force men. That afternoon all the Air Force men at the base, including Father, were taken away to an undisclosed location where they were tortured as investigations began. Three weeks later, with no word about the men, we were evicted from the base. It was an odd feeling, to move out of the base in such an unexpected way. I could tell Mother was concerned about Father, but she never talked about her feelings.

In the same way, Margy and I did not talk about anything relating to the emotional effect of Father being gone. I felt some relief, knowing that I wouldn't have to deal with his discipline as long as he was away. Aware that many of the neighbors' children missed their fathers, I felt guilty for not being overly sad about his absence. I knew I should miss him, but even though I did not want him to die, it felt good to have a break from his violent rages. On the other hand, it meant that Mother would now be the only one to deal with our shortcomings, and the hurtful words she used when angry with us were often even more painful than the beatings we endured from Father. This combination of conflicting emotions led to an inner turmoil that I couldn't express. Unfortunately, the one thing I did know was that I hated him, and Mother too.

Lydia's wedding came and went without Father. I went back to school in September, and Mother and Margy moved to a one-room apartment in one of the low income neighborhoods. We had no idea how long it would be before we could resume the normal life we had known at the Air Force base. The more I thought about Father, the more I found myself wondering what difference he really made in my life. For years, I had longed to feel loved by him, but instead, thoughts about him led to fear and resentment. Now I wondered what it would be like in the following months, not having him in my life. How different would his absence have felt if I had ever been loved by him? What was it really like to be loved by any man? *Would a boyfriend meet that need in me?*

Chapter 10

THE TEEN CHALLENGE

As the third term progressed, I found myself more focused on what it would feel like to have a boy pay attention to me. My grades had been declining steadily since I had lost motivation to do well. My academic success had not mattered to Mother and Father. With little interest in my school work, watching classmates play the dating game became my favorite pastime. I envied the girls with boyfriends. Surely I didn't have what it took to be part of their world, having believed what Mother and Father said about me. Yet deep inside I longed to be wanted, and I even noticed the good-looking boys.

I was clueless as to how I would even respond if any of them showed an interest in me. Then Jeff the basketball coach, a tall and handsome light-skinned gentleman, swept me off my feet when he invited me

He Really Is My Father

to a game one evening. I fumbled sheepishly with the ball as he tried to show me how to shoot a basket. His sweet smelling aftershave filled the air as I followed him around the basketball court, attempting to keep up with his moves. I was so awed by his charm that my knees felt weak. Afterwards, all I could do was become obsessed with the fantasy of becoming his girlfriend someday. He had noticed me.

December holidays came, and I went to be with Mother and Margy. I familiarized myself with the surroundings of the new neighborhood. Mother slept on the only bed in the one room that was now our home. The bed was separated from the main living area, where she had neatly arranged four stools and a small coffee table by a curtain made out of an old bed sheet. The small sink facing the one window in the room was only to be used for drawing cooking water. Everything else had to be done at the communal washing area. The bathroom was also shared with seven other households, which meant that no one really took responsibility for keeping it clean. Unaccustomed to such filthy conditions, I took it upon myself to thoroughly clean the toilet each morning, so I could at least tolerate using it once a day. Mother was still quarrelsome and continued to find fault in everything we did. I couldn't wait to go back to school.

One evening, on my way to the store, I ran into an old face from grade school. Karume, the very boy who had sent me a love note in standard five, recognized me.

The Teen Challenge

As we shared memories from our elementary days, feeling so grown up at age 14, I learned that he lived in our neighborhood. I showed him where we lived, convinced that the one incident so long ago was far behind us and had no bearing on our present lives. To my surprise, Karume showed up at our window later that evening. Had I failed to tell him that Mother was very hostile to any friendships we had, especially those of the other gender? When I had listened to girls talk about boys throwing stones at the window to get the girls' attention when their parents were home, it had sounded so romantic. But now, as Karume insistently waved at me just outside our window, it was anything but romantic. Mother, who happened to be sitting on the bed with the curtain pulled aside, saw him and became outraged.

"Who is that?" she asked impatiently.

I stammered, attempting to explain that Karume was a former classmate I had just happened to run into earlier that evening. I should have known better than to try and reason with Mother. Not even waiting for me to finish explaining, she stormed out of the house and made her way around the building to the place where Karume was standing. Walking toward him, she lashed out and threatened to throw him out of our neighborhood.

"What do you think you are doing, seducing my daughter right in front of me?" I heard her ask.

Karume walked away hurriedly, almost as though he had anticipated trouble. The difference between this and the stories shared by the girls at school was that I had no interest in Karume. I still dreamed of Jeff and intended to save my heart for him, for I was convinced he would be the one to rescue me from all my misery. Mother came back to the house still raging in anger.

"I knew boarding school was a mistake," she yelled. "Now you think you can seduce boys right in front of me? You have no shame. If you get pregnant I will send you away. Do you understand? You think you can prostitute yourself in my house? If I ever see you with a boy again, I will send you away."

I stood in silence as she continued to vent. Margy looked confused, but she pretended to be busy in order to avoid getting into any trouble herself. Mother was right about one thing. Boarding school had changed me, although not in the ways she imagined. I was beginning to think there could be a way out of this miserable life. Having experienced life outside of this home, I began to consider other possibilities. That night I made up my mind that I wouldn't take Mother's treatment anymore. When Mother left for work the following morning, I packed my suitcase and told Margy I was leaving.

"Where are you going?" she asked, sounding alarmed. I wondered if she had ever entertained the thought of running away. She didn't really have anyone. In some ways, I didn't have anyone either, but now, having met my sisters and knowing where my brother David lived, I hoped that if I could explain what life was like with Mother, someone would rescue me.

"To BuruBuru where David lives," I answered confidently. The confidence was not based on the certainty that things would work out. But I had decided that I would somehow reclaim what Mother and Father had taken away from me—my family.

I could tell that Margy wanted to ask more questions, but she was stunned by my announcement. I wished I could take her with me, but I didn't even know if I would be allowed to stay with David. At this point, I was even prepared to live on the street if I needed to. Anything was better than living with Mother. Looking in Margy's now teary eyes, I said goodbye and left.

Two weeks went by, and all seemed to be going so well that I wished I had made my escape sooner. Mother had not come looking for me, and no one had really asked me why I had run away. But soon after the two weeks, my real sister Margy came. She informed me that we were to visit Lydia, who lived in a suburb on the south side of the city. I knew right away that the purpose of this trip was to talk about my escape. I had no idea what to expect. After supper, I went to the kitchen to do the dishes. And then, strategically, Lydia came into the kitchen to help with the clean up.

"Why did you run away?" she asked hesitantly.

I had expected the question and even prepared my answer. It was time to tell someone about my suffering. I was convinced that once I laid my case, no one would want to send me back to the cruel life I had endured for years. I would start by explaining the most recent injustice, and then I would tell them about the beatings and mistreatment that Margy and I had suffered. I hoped Lydia would be outraged enough to demand that Margy be removed from that home as well. But when I opened my mouth, the words that came out weren't as compelling as I desired. It was difficult to articulate the experience of my lost childhood. The confidence I had felt when running away two weeks earlier was suddenly replaced by a sense of inadequacy. The echo of self-doubt caused me to question the validity of my accusation, so that when I heard the words leave my mouth, I found myself wondering—was Mother really wrong in claiming I was a bad girl? I had, after all, fantasized about a boy! The following day, Margy took me back to Mother's.

I turned fifteen the following June and was feeling more grown up than ever. I was still infatuated with Jeff, who had still not paid me any more attention. I spent weeks thinking about him and wondering what it would be like to be loved by him. And then, when we broke off for the August holidays, I met Tom. He had caught my eye when a classmate and I were sitting on a porch in the neighborhood. Tom had passed by riding his bike, and I had followed him with my eyes. He was drop-dead gorgeous. My classmate, more experienced when it came to matters relating to boys, noticed my interest and arranged for Tom to meet me. Tom and I spent many afternoons together, taking great care not to be caught. I would do the house chores in the mornings. Then after lunch, taking advantage of Mother's convenient schedule, I would go to Tom's house and make it back home by four, just before Mother came back. Tom and I would listen to music and talk about our idealistic future, a dream home and good jobs. I never spoke of my life at home. After my experience with Lydia after running away, I wasn't convinced I was justified in complaining about my life. My only hope now was escaping through marriage some day, just like Lydia. One afternoon, however, during my usual visits with Tom, things took a different turn.

"Close your eyes," he had said, smiling. Since Tom was the first boy who really paid me the kind of attention I had longed for, I didn't question anything he did or said. I enjoyed this young love with a trust I had not known for years. With my eyes closed, I leaned toward him as he pulled me toward the end of the room and made me sit at the edge of the bed.

"Can I open my eyes now?" I asked, wondering what the surprise would be.

"Yes. Let's sleep here."

His words hit me like a slap across my face.

"What?"

I could not believe what he was suggesting. I didn't have to be boy-smart to understand what was being implied. We had never talked about sex, but I knew in my heart that it was not to be part of any relationship of mine. Abstaining from sex wasn't even due to the fear of becoming pregnant. It was just something I knew I shouldn't do. I quickly started to walk away, afraid to be contaminated by his distasteful gesture.

"I thought you wanted it," he said apologetically.

"What made you think that?" I asked angrily, feeling already defiled by the mere thought of him touching me in that manner. I then hurried toward the door to leave his place. Even though he apologized, I knew I never wanted to see him again.

It wasn't until I was seventeen that I met my next boyfriend. I had completed my secondary school exams and was now living with Lydia and her husband Peter. A decision had been made for me to move out of Mother's house after Father had been released from prison. I had not been part of the decision, but I had heard that it had been a financial one. Mother, who had initially asked me to forget about my family, had now turned to the same people I was supposed to forget, because I had become too expensive.

The process of changing the course of my life without my input had reminded me of the day I was separated from my family after Mama's death. While I was glad to be out of Mother's home, I didn't feel like dreams about my future were ever taken into consideration. No one had asked me what I wanted to do with my life. I had had no part in the decision. Furthermore, I had also been forced to enroll in a tailoring school, a skill I had no interest in. But even if they had asked me what I wanted to do, I couldn't have answered because I didn't know. I had given up trying to win approval and with that, I made no effort to develop goals for myself. What I cared about had not mattered for years, so I had stopped having my own thoughts, at least not enough to be able to express them. And with that approach to life, I let others guide me even when I hated the choices they made. It was during my time at the tailoring school that I noticed the boy next door.

From the moment Martin paid attention to me, I knew Peter and Lydia wouldn't approve. My reasoning was that no one ever approved of me, so anything I cared about was not permissible. Martin was in his early thirties, just like Peter, so when he asked if his age would matter to my sister I said no, even though I had intended to keep the relationship a secret. His age wasn't the reason for my need to be secretive about our relationship. I was just scared of doing anything on my own. I was scared of having thoughts, opinions, or preferences. When asked if I preferred coffee or tea, I didn't know what to say. And because of this fear, I told a lot of lies. On my first date with Martin, when I gave my reason for leaving the house, I told Lydia I was going to see a friend from college.

Phew! That was easy, I had thought as I quickly made my exit before Lydia could change her mind. A few minutes later, I had knocked on Martin's front door, only two houses away. As I waited patiently, I had constantly looked over my shoulder, afraid that Lydia or Peter would see me. After that day, Martin and I continued to spend many weekends together listening to music and occasionally going to the movies, all done very carefully so I wouldn't be caught, or so I hoped. One Sunday evening, Lydia informed me that she and Peter wanted to have a talk with me.

"We are aware you have been seeing Martin," Peter spoke in a firm tone. I was shocked. How could they possibly know? My mind raced to incidents where I may have been careless. Our relationship had progressed to seeing each other even on weekdays, taking advantage of my trips to the nearby market. Was it possible that I had been spotted? Was I taking too long when running errands?

"We would like you to stop seeing him," Peter said, interrupting my thoughts. I was stunned. *What! Why... Why do they always ruin my fun? Why does everything I enjoy always have to come to an end? God, do you hate me this much?* I was slowly beginning to blame God for everything that happened to me.

The Teen Challenge

"If you ever get pregnant we will send you away," Peter continued. I stared at him in disbelief. Everyone seemed to be so obsessed with pregnancy. While I didn't have much of a mind of my own, there were some choices I made. And I resented the fact that everyone seemed to assume the worst when it came to boys. I hated this assumption so much that I wished I could really get pregnant just to get back at them. If only I knew how. If only I had the courage to even let Martin hold me close. He once told me that I seemed to be afraid of intimacy.

What was intimacy? I had no idea. Each time he pulled me toward him, I had always stiffened, he said. And now I was being threatened about being sent away if there was pregnancy, just like Mother had warned. I wanted to laugh sarcastically, but instead, I nodded in agreement, staring blankly in the space between Lydia and Peter. They really didn't know me. I even questioned if they had any interest in understanding me. I couldn't even look at Lydia because I felt betrayed by her. She was supposed to be my sister, yet the only evidence for this relationship was the physical resemblance. We were such strangers.

When the speech was over, I hurried toward my room, wondering how Martin would take the news. And I wondered how I would take the separation as well. I needed the relationship, because he made me feel special. I was *visible* to him.

Chapter 11

Plateau

Martin and I saw each other secretly for another year. I was caught a few times and lied my way out. Then, sometime in 1987 my time in Nairobi came to an abrupt end, when another decision was made for me. Against my will, I was to move to Eldoret where Judy and my real sister Margy lived. My relationship with Martin did not survive long distance, and he was quickly replaced by Joe, a boyfriend I met at a Bible camp. I had become involved with Navigators, an interdenominational organization whose mission is to know Christ and to make Him known, and through them, I had come to understand more about assurance of salvation. Joe, who had seemed like a nice guy, turned out to be like Tom, and he ended our relationship by simply saying sex was very important to men.

Unable to find the fulfillment I was looking for in boys, my activities now included Bible studies and weekly meetings with a friend also involved with the Navigators. Her name was Sara, and she helped me grow in my relationship with Jesus by providing accountability and teaching me simple spiritual disciplines such as the importance of God's word through personal Bible reading and Scripture memorization. I struggled with the father aspect of God, never having had a positive father figure in my life. Sara and I spent most of our times together talking about why God seemed to be against me. Sara patiently listened and tried to tell me that God was really on my side, but it was easier to blame Him for all that had gone wrong in my life.

Aunt Josephine, whose wedding we had attended two weeks before Mama's death, had also moved to Eldoret, and she and I became good friends and visited often. At nineteen, I was getting tired of not knowing how to answer questions regarding my background, so one afternoon I decided to ask Aunt Josephine about my father. Mama's answer to me when I was five was no longer enough. I needed more information.

"When did my father die?"

"In 1959."

1959? Either I am wrong about my age, or this man was not my father. I couldn't decide what was worse, to be wrong about my age or my father. I decided to clarify my age, and when Aunt Josephine confirmed what I knew to be true, I felt nauseated. The man Mama had led me to believe was my father—dead as he might be—was not my father. I felt dizzy. As I reached for the kitchen chair to sit down, Aunt Josephine sensed I was in shock. She held out her hand to keep me from falling.

"You don't know anything about this, right?" she asked, looking embarrassed, as if she had just disclosed information she was not supposed to.

"No. Can you please explain?" My voice was rising and I felt exasperated. She took a seat next to me and moved closer before holding my hand. Then she began to speak so gently.

"Your mother was married to my brother Zephania in 1954," she said as I stared at her, wondering what I was about to learn.

"She then had your sister Lydia in 1955, and Judy in 1956. She suffered a miscarriage in 1957 and gave birth to your sister Margy in 1959. Your mother and my brother loved each other very much. In fact, they used to call each other darling, something that was not very common in Kenya back then. My brother worked for East African Airways at the time, and they lived in Nairobi. Unfortunately, he was killed in a tragic car accident while driving home to visit our parents." She paused, obviously reliving the sadness of losing a brother so young. It hurt to think Mama had been widowed so early in her marriage. I could not imagine how she had managed to raise the children. Then more curiously, I wanted to know how my brother and I came to be.

"Then what happened?" I prompted.

"After the funeral, your mother was asked to marry one of my brothers, as was the custom back then," she continued. "The practice was that, if a woman was widowed young, she was to be married to one of her brothers-in-law, so she could continue to bear children for the family. But your mother was educated, and a Christian, and did not agree with the tradition. She was also not even attracted to any of her brothers-in-law. When she refused, she became alienated from our family."

"How did she end up at your wedding then?" I asked, wondering why she would be telling me all these things when she was part of that family.

"Your mother and I were very good friends, and I also didn't believe in the custom. I continued to visit her even though my family did not approve."

She paused for a moment. I was still curious about David and me and needed to know about my father. This was the critical missing piece in my life, the only hole that still ached with emptiness. Even though Mother had been cruel, I had enjoyed my own Mama's love. But since I had never had a man really love me like Mama did, Father's cruelty had left me seeking for that emotional connection that only a man can give, or so I thought. Boyfriends had been so temporary, and lately I was beginning to demand that God give me a permanent man who could be just mine. I believed he owed me that much. As it dawned on me that there might be a man out there who could be my father, I felt a gleam of hope that there was someone somewhere for me.

"Your mother moved back home to live with her parents, because she could not afford to live in Nairobi anymore," Aunt Josephine continued. "She took a teaching job and met a man who then became David's father." Noticing that she referred to this man as David's father, I became impatient. I desperately needed to know about *my* father.

"How about me?" I demanded.

"Your story is very different. After your brother was born, your mother found another teaching job far from where her parents lived. She then moved, taking David with her. Later it became difficult to look after David on her own so she sent for Margy."

She continued to talk unhurriedly despite my obvious impatience. I learned that when Mama had gone to pick Margy up from the bus stop, Margy had not been there. Since it had been too late to walk back home, Mama had taken refuge at a pastor's house. Something about the way she said this part caused me to sit up in anticipation for the news about my father. She then hesitated before going on.

"And…?" I urged her to continue.

"Unfortunately, it turned out that the pastor's wife was not around." She stopped. Was I supposed to come to some conclusion?

"And…?" I urged her again.

"The pastor took advantage of your mother."

"You mean he raped her?" No longer enthralled by her suspense, I was direct.

My dizziness returned. *This can't be true. I do not want to be a product of rape. I want a daddy, not a rapist.*

I couldn't listen to Aunt Josephine anymore. I had heard enough. I rose from my seat and went to the bathroom, where I sobbed like a child for several minutes. I hated Aunt Josephine for being the bearer of such news. I wanted her to be wrong, yet I couldn't think of any reason why she would come up with such a dreadful story. Then I heard her knock on the bathroom door.

"Are you OK?" she asked.

I opened the door, not sure how I was supposed to relate to her, having just learned that her brother was not really my father, which meant that technically, I was not her niece. I wanted to be alone. I made up a story about a friend I needed to see. But as she said goodbye, a sudden heaviness descended upon me, making me wonder whether I really wanted her to go yet. She was my only link to the truth about my history at that moment. I wondered if talking about Mama with her would reveal more about what I really was dying to know—the whereabouts of my biological father. But the stubbornness and determination to fix what I considered to be my problem made me decide against asking her to stay. I closed the door behind her and went to my bedroom where I lay down and cried myself to sleep.

By the following morning, I had made up my mind to search for my father. I believed that if he were still alive, there was a chance I could have a family—a real family with a real father. So, I decided I would start my search with Plateau Hospital, where Mama had died.

The bus ride to Plateau lasted about an hour. When the driver told me we had arrived, I thought it was a mistake. The place looked so different from what I remembered about the day after Mama had died. All I could see now was farmland, with nothing that looked like a hospital.

"Where is the hospital?" I asked the driver. He pointed in a far away direction that still didn't reveal anything.

"Take that path you see right there and walk for about fifteen minutes," an elderly man sitting nearby added. I took the dirt path and walked for twenty-five minutes, before finally arriving at the hospital gates and proceeded to an administrative office. Although I expected to cry at the sight of the hospital, which would inevitably bring back memories of Mama's death, I felt nothing. It was as though my feelings had become frozen, so that even though I knew this had been the start of years of endless pain, my heart did not give way to any emotions. Only the night before, I had cried myself to sleep. And now, facing the very spot where Mama's life had ended, nothing happened.

A voice of greeting from behind a desk startled me.

"Good morning. Uhm, I need some help," I stumbled as I made my way forward. Behind the desk was a wall lined with huge filing cabinets. I strained my neck to try and read the labels on the cabinets, wondering if this was where records were kept.

"What can I do for you?" the man behind the desk asked.

"Well, I hope you can help me. My mother died in this hospital in 1975, and I need some information about the cause of her death." That didn't come out very well, and it certainly wasn't what I really wanted to know. But it was going to have to do for the time being, with the hope that somewhere in that information would be some a clue as to who my father had been.

"Sorry madam, we don't keep records that far back. Everything is destroyed after seven years. It's been 13 years since…"

I sighed. I couldn't believe I had come all this way to find nothing. I felt stupid. Deciding there was no use to try to find my father, I started to walk away.

"You wouldn't even want to see the archives room. There are probably rats in there," the man behind the desk spoke, stopping me in my tracks.

"The archives?"

"Yes. It is so full of old records, there are probably lots of big rats in there, busy multiplying themselves." I smiled, feeling very lucky all of a sudden. I managed to convince him to give me the keys, and thanked him profusely as I hurried in the direction he had sent me. I even entertained the thought that God was possibly watching over me. But I didn't dare dwell on the thought too long in case it would give him reason to frustrate my plans.

After unlocking the door, I walked in and ran my hand across the wall for a light switch. I looked around to see if there were any rats. The place was so quiet that it almost felt spooky. There were so many shelves loaded with files, I didn't even know where to begin. The files were not organized chronologically or alphabetically, which made the process needlessly long. After searching for what seemed like hours, I finally came across a section with files from 1975. Minutes later, I found Mama's file.

I stared at the file for a long time before opening it, wondering why I seemed to lack any of the expected feelings. I had been certain that seeing a file with her name on it, tangible evidence that she once really lived, would trigger painful memories, but I just sat there. I missed her more than I had in a long time, but that was all. I was holding something that spoke of her existence, but life with her now felt like so long ago.

I opened the file and, to my disappointment, there was only a copy of her death record stating the cause of her death. What had I expected? Isn't that what I had said to the man at the front desk—that I needed to know the cause of Mama's death? About that time, I realized I didn't really know what I was looking for. No one had ever told me anything about where I was born. Besides, chances were Mama had never disclosed my father's name at the hospital anyway. More information would be needed before I could try to trace my father. Perhaps if there were any missionaries still working at the hospital, there was a chance they might know something about my father. I quickly took the copy out of the file, convincing myself that it was OK to take it since they didn't keep records that far back, and went back to the front desk.

The man informed me that there was a Dutch nurse who still worked at the hospital. Her name was Marie. Confirming that she was not on duty, the man gave me directions to her house. With my heart racing, I walked to her apartment and knocked at her door, desperately hoping she would be in. It was getting late and I needed to hurry back before nightfall.

"Come in!" she said, opening the door. She offered me tea and asked where I had come from. She was easy to chat with, and in our conversation I learned that the Bouws were still connected with the Dutch Mission organization. She gave me their contact information and sent me on my way. This was more than I had expected. The Bouws had been Mama's closest friends. I was certain they would have information regarding my father. I was getting close to finding the piece that had been missing in my life.

But when I told Sara what I was thinking, she had a different opinion. She convinced me it was probably not a good idea to try and find my father, suggesting that possibly the man had never told his family about Mama, and probably didn't even want to know me. Not wanting to face more rejection, I agreed with her. But I still wanted to at least get in touch with the Bouws, just to know if they remembered me, and hopefully make one more connection to my past.

Chapter 12

I Fly Away

I wrote two letters: one to my sister Lydia, asking her to give me her account of my birth, and the other to the Bouws. The response from Lydia came sooner than I expected. In it, she explained Mama's rape in the same way Aunt Josephine had. She also added that the rape had been so violent that Mama almost lost her life in the process. Mama had then reported the matter to the Bouws, since they were the directors of the Dutch Mission in the district where the pastor's church was. Even though the matter went to court, in those days the law didn't protect women against such violence, and Mama had lost the case. The argument was that she had gone to the man's house, implying that she was asking for it. The Bouws, being sympathetic toward Mama, moved her to Eldoret and gave her a job at the Center. The man was asked to leave the parish.

A week later, I received a response from Mr. Wim Bouw. It was evident they remembered me and were very happy to hear from me. In fact, Wim encouraged me to write again, expressing that if there was anything they could do to help in any way, I should let them know. As I read the last line of the letter, my eyes moistened as my throat chocked with emotion. I could not remember ever reading the words Wim used to end the letter. *I love you,* he had written.

Hearing these words from a man who had no reason to love me was deeply moving. I held onto the letter and read it over and over again. I remembered how, as a little girl, I had often played outside the Bouws' home along with their children, oblivious to any differences there might have been between us. They had treated me like part of their family. The letter brought such comfort. If I could just keep the precious memories of those early years of my life when everything was perfect, perhaps I could resurrect my sense of self-worth. Maybe it was possible that if I experienced the joy of feeling loved again just for being me, I could smile without the ache that followed soon after the curve lines on my cheeks faded. Back in those days I had mattered—not just to Mama, but also to the Bouws. I was going to write again.

When I received a second letter from Wim, encouraging me as he had in the first one, it dawned on me that God may have really gone before me when I made the trip to Plateau Hospital. Instead of finding what I thought I was looking for, I had become reconnected with a man who had at one time felt like a father to me. In my next letter, I asked if I could call him Daddy.

Daddy and I wrote back and forth, talking about life. I found myself telling him things that I had never before discussed with anyone. I shared about my dreams to go to college some day, about boys, and even my desire to get married. In his responses he shared wisdom and insight as only a father can. Each time he also conveyed greetings from Mommy, reminding me that she, too, loved me. In 1991 I received news that I had only imagined I might ever receive; Mommy and Daddy were intending to come to Kenya. I could not believe there was a chance I would see them again. Even though their primary visit was related to the mission, the fact that they planned to see me made me feel very special. While I had told my sisters about my reconnection with the Bouws, I had not shared anything about the parental relationship that was developing through the letters. Lydia and her husband had by now moved to Eldoret where they had opened a medical practice. My sisters and I had still not reached the level of talking about personal matters. The distance created by our long separation had left no room for an intimate relationship. In fact, in my mind, I was still trapped in the mode of not being allowed to think of them as my sisters. The discovery that we didn't share a father only served to further alienate me from them. So, when talking about Mommy and Daddy, I found myself referring to them as the Bouws. It was also possible that I was afraid my sisters would forbid me from relating to them in that way. So much had been snatched from me that I wasn't about to take a chance. But dutifully, I informed them of the Bouws' planned visit. When they finally arrived in May, my sisters and I gathered at Lydia's house to meet them.

Daddy's smile had not changed a bit and, when I looked into his eyes, I knew he saw me in exactly the same way he had when they had been our neighbors at the Center. Words were not necessary—I was his daughter. I met them one more time when they visited my boutique. Using my new tailoring skills, acquired when I had lived with Lydia in Nairobi, I had opened a boutique, Excel Fashions.

Two months later, a day after my 23rd birthday, I walked into my shop and was rudely greeted by a sight I will never forget. My boutique had been broken into and everything had been stolen. Devastated, I ran to the only people I hoped to get help from, my sisters. Somehow, they blamed me for what had happened, claiming I had not been careful. They did not offer me any practical help. I had very little money to begin with, and that went into paying back the clients whose clothes had been stolen in the break-in. It was unlikely that I could continue with the business. I then wrote to Daddy, because I needed to tell someone who would care.

In response to my letter, Daddy invited me to consider going to Holland, with the possibility of attending college. This was an offer I had never dreamed of. I accepted it, and on December 14, 1991, I boarded an airplane at Jomo Kenyatta International Airport, to begin a new life that would change me forever.

Chapter 13

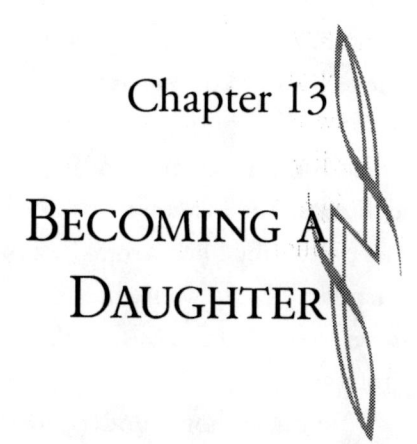

BECOMING A DAUGHTER

My plane touched down at Schipol Airport the following morning at 6:00 a.m., two hours behind Kenyan time. Following the signs to customs, I waited in line along with several other visitors. I handed my passport to the customs official at the desk. He flipped through the pages in search of my entry visa.

"What brings you to Holland?" he asked with a distinctive Dutch accent.

"I am visiting friends." I knew saying parents, even though I had the urge to do so, would raise unnecessary questions that I was not prepared to answer.

"Are they waiting for you?"

Anne Marijke and Gisbert were waiting for me because, since it was a Sunday, Daddy was preaching. After becoming reacquainted, we took the train to Ede where they lived with the rest of the Bouw family. The rich aroma of the strong Dutch coffee that welcomed me as I walked in was deceptive, as the bitter taste was nothing like the Kahawa I was used to in Kenya. But when Mommy asked what I thought of it, I said it was delicious. She asked about my trip, and I politely told her everything I believed to be appropriate to say on the first day. I badly wanted to talk about how hard it had been to convince my sisters that I wasn't running away from anything.

No one at home understood how much the Bouw family had come to mean to me in the three years before my departure to join them. How could I explain the way Daddy filled the father shaped hole in my heart, when I had never expressed my deep sense of abandonment to the very people who had forsaken me? I had held it against my sisters for not rescuing me, when we had driven away from the Center in the grey Zephyr that took me to my long desolate life. I was angry at them for not knowing what it was like to live with Mother and Father. I hated them for living their lives as though Mama's death had not scarred them in the same way it had scarred me. And they could never convince me that they understood what it felt like not to know who my father was; they had known their own father.

I wanted to pour out all this built up anger to Mommy because she had known Mama, and in some ways could be like Mama. I wanted Mommy to hold me the same way Mama used to hold me even though, at age 23, I was far too big for a lap. But I knew better than to blurt out all my emotions. I had learned to guard my heart, especially with strangers.

Yes, Mommy still felt like a stranger. Even though Daddy had constantly assured me that she loved me, it was Daddy who wrote me. Through his letters, I had come to know his heart. His sincerity spoke through each word and each line, which was why I had felt an instant connection when we had met in person only seven months earlier. Or was it simply that, to me, he resembled the piece that had been missing in my life? Feeling jet-lagged, I was relieved when Mommy finally released me for an afternoon nap. And in the days that followed, that sense of relief seemed to accompany me each time I left Mommy's presence. I always preferred to be with Daddy instead.

In addition to being a pastor, Daddy worked with the home office of the Dutch Mission organization that sent skilled professionals to different countries to work in developing communities. The office was located in a small town called Zeist. To pass time, Daddy invited me to help at the office with some clerical duties—a good opportunity to equip me with some much needed skills. I had never touched a computer before, and he, with his gentle nature, guided me ever so carefully around a word processor. Within weeks, I was typing most of his letters.

There were, however, other less obvious skills that I needed to learn. One of them had presented an opportunity on my first day to work with him. While I finished my breakfast, Daddy had proceeded to prepare sandwiches for lunch. As he worked on the two sandwiches, even though I thought I had heard him say they were for both of us, I could not bring myself to allow anyone to serve me. So I took my place by the counter and began to make a sandwich, copying everything I saw him do as an extra precaution. After all, I wouldn't want to make a sandwich incorrectly.

"You need more than one sandwich?" he asked politely, pushing the lunchmeat toward me. Not sure what to say, I smiled sheepishly. I was so tense I could hardly spread the butter on the bread. I started working on the second sandwich only because he had made two. I did exactly what he did. He then packed the four sandwiches and two apples before driving us to work. At lunch time, we sat at the table with a few of Daddy's colleagues, and as everyone brought out their sandwiches, it dawned on me that one sandwich per person was typically enough. If the lesson was for me to let others do things for me, I was a long way from mastering that skill. And in addition to that, the fact that I was accustomed to being invisible meant that at the house, I ate in silence, sat in silence, and only answered questions when asked, a habit that drove Mommy and others at the house crazy.

By February, with my visa soon to expire, Daddy chose to send me to England to apply for a re-entry visa at the embassy in London. He made arrangements for me to attend a discipleship school for a month. This was to also serve as a way to give me something to do while he worked on my college plans. My experience with decisions made for me against my will in the past made it difficult for me to trust Daddy. So, while in England, I chose to visit schools to check things out for myself. At the discipleship school, I also had an opportunity to go through an exercise that helped me discover my strengths and interests. It was through this exercise that I became attracted to economics.

By the time I returned to Holland in March, I had set my heart to go to the University of Leicester to study Business Economics. As I waited for school to start, Daddy and I spent many hours together on the road. In addition to the drive to work twice a week, he took me to several churches where he preached as a guest. I discovered many different parts of Holland, just as much as I discovered many aspects of becoming a daughter. As he allowed me to open my heart to him, the acceptance I felt brought me closer to being able to trust him as a daughter would.

The more comfortable I became around Daddy, the harder it was to relate to Mommy. I was spending so much of my energy soaking in the kind of love I had needed all my life, that I made no room for a relationship with Mommy. It was not that I didn't want to be close to her; I just didn't know what kind of relationship I needed to have with her. Like a jigsaw puzzle piece, Daddy had a perfect spot, and the picture was complete with no room for Mommy. But how could I express that?

Tension continued to build between Mommy and me. I was unable to include her in my now complete life, and she was confused by my inability to relate to her. When the time came for me to go to school, I was again relieved to be away from her. By the end of the school year, Daddy found himself caught between two warring women—Mommy, feeling rejected by me and troubled by my closeness to Daddy, and me, unable to let Mommy into my life. He had to take Mommy's side.

"You will not be going back to Leicester next year," he began the evening before I was to leave for Kenya for the summer break. It had been so easy for me to ask him if I could go visit my family. I had truly become Daddy's girl and pretty much received anything I asked for. In my opinion, he was the world's best Daddy. But that night, as he spoke those unexpected words to me, I could not believe my ears. On second thought, it had actually been too good to be real. *Wasn't it more typical for things to always go wrong in my life? Wasn't it normal for everything I cared about to be taken from me? I should have known my life in Holland would come to an end sooner or later.*

BECOMING A DAUGHTER

Looking at Daddy as he spoke that night, all I could hear was that everything I had known for the last year-and-a-half was being taken away from me. And now, instead of a continuous tape reminding me of my unworthiness, in my mind I saw what looked like a slow motion movie with scenes of the things I had lost from Mama's death; the Zephyr pulling away from the Center, to all the gifts being taken away from me over the years, and Martin. On this night, the loss was my education.

"Why are you doing this to me Daddy?"

"Doing what?" he asked, shocked by my reaction.

"Taking everything away from me? Don't you know how much I love Leicester? Why did you bring me here to experience this, only to take it away? This is not fair. It would have been better if you had not let me experience any of it at all." My voice was shaking as I spoke. I was so angry with him, and with God for all the wrongs in my life.

"I think you are misunderstanding me. Can you listen for a moment?" Daddy interrupted, gently as always.

"You just told me that you are sending me back home for good. Did any of this mean anything to you? Calling me daughter and showing me around, telling everybody how smart I was?"

"I don't remember saying your education or my relationship with you was over. All I was saying is, Leicester is very expensive, and we would like to find you a cheaper school here in Holland, but it might take time because we also need to raise funds for your education. So, I was asking if you could wait in Kenya until the school was found, and then you could come back."

And then he dropped the real bombshell.

"Mommy also finds it a bit difficult…"

The rest became muted. All I could see were his lips moving.

When I got on my flight the next morning, I had my mind made up. I would not trust anyone again. I would go to Kenya because the ticket had already been purchased, but once there, I would call the airlines and schedule my return flight. I would utilize the few contacts I had in Holland and England, and without anymore communication with the Bouws, I would find my own way of paying for school in Leicester, complete my education and be on my own.

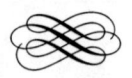

Three-and-a-half weeks later, I was back in Leicester, having had to fly to Schipol first. A friend had picked me up at the airport, and a day later I had taken the ferry to England. I spent that week visiting different organizations searching for ways to fund my education. In the meantime, the friend in Holland had thought it fair to inform Daddy of my return. At the end of that week I received a letter from Daddy, expressing disappointment in my action. He asked if I considered them to be such bad people that I couldn't even talk to them about my intentions. At the same time he said he understood my desire to continue with my studies and wished me all the best.

It was not easy to learn that I had disappointed the man who had given so much to me. How could I have been so self-centered? I simply didn't know how to be anything else. Every decision I made was based on a need to protect myself. I was the only person I could trust, since I had been let down so many times. But seeing how my actions had affected Daddy, I felt ashamed. There was no denying that I had done wrong. But was it possible to go back to how things had been?

I continued to work at finding a way to go back to school. In my mind, there was no way Daddy would take on the huge responsibility of funding the education of someone who had proved to be ungrateful. Through years of receiving everything with strings attached, I had learned that once I messed up, there was no forgiveness, and all privileges would be lost.

When I had arrived at the Harwich International Port in England, I had been asked about my financial status and how I planned to fund my education. The thing about being naive is that you don't lie to authorities. I had said I didn't have any money—not a good answer for any immigration official. This had automatically granted me only a few weeks of legal stay until I could prove I had funding. I had gone ahead and registered for classes at the university, believing I would find a way to pay for school before the fall term was over. The student services office gave me a room at the university housing where I had previously stayed. They also gave me a letter that allowed me to receive a work permit, enabling me to extend my stay in the country. And so I took a job at a chips factory where I worked the night shift. Sleeping during the day, I successfully avoided my classmates and other friends, who knew nothing about my situation. How could I explain to them that I had thrown away everything by having let Mommy and Daddy down?

To my surprise, Daddy did not give up on me. I received another letter from him with information about a school he had found for me. It was a bit late for the fall term, but he said if I was interested, the next term started in February. A second letter came from Holland. It was from Mommy, and in it she was asking for forgiveness for how she had treated me during my stay in Holland. This was the first letter I ever received from her. I never imagined a letter from her would be like this. No one had ever considered me worthy enough to ask for my forgiveness. And so, in February 1994, like a prodigal daughter, I showed up at the doorstep of the Bouw's home.

Chapter 14

GRONINGEN

The sun was shining in Utrecht that Saturday morning when I arrived. It was as though God's face was glowing down upon me as Daddy and I hugged at the doorstep. I hesitated at first, waiting for a sign that all was well. On the ferry from England, I had tried to rehearse a perfect speech that would guarantee reconciliation. The letters I had received during the five months after rebelliously going back to Leicester had not quite convinced me that there would be no consequences for my behavior. I wanted to earn their trust again. Through my words, I would show them that I was sorry for what I had done, and I would promise to be a better child if only they could give me a second chance. When I looked into Daddy's eyes, the speech became instantly unnecessary. I knew everything had been put behind us, and this was to be a new beginning. Crossing the threshold was like entering into the new life I had experienced the day I had asked Jesus into my heart back in high school. A load of guilt had been lifted off my shoulders.

As we hauled boxes packed with kitchen utensils, beddings and food onto a trailer later that afternoon, it was Daddy who bore the weight of my new life. I was moving to Groningen, where I would study business at one of the very few international universities in the country. After we arrived, Daddy helped me unpack and set up my room, one of three in a student apartment where I was to live with two other girls. He then sat down and shared a meal prepared by one of my new roommates, enjoying every moment as though nothing had ever come between us. The contrast to the life I had lived under Mother and Father was unbelievable. This was true forgiveness.

But even with such an abundance of love being lavishly poured upon me, I was to discover that receiving love was sometimes just as difficult as not having any love at all. Soon after settling into my new routine, I joined the local Navigator Bible Study group. As the cold February wind coming down from the North Sea pierced through my tropical skin, I spent very little time outside. The Navigator Bible Study group meetings on the weekend became my only social outlet. At school, everyone seemed to mind their own business and as a result, with my main contacts being back in Kenya, I incurred an enormous phone bill. That led to another test of my ability to receive love. How could I bring myself to tell Daddy that I had just messed up again? In my world, you didn't make mistakes. All wrongdoing was severely punished, and nothing could be worse than having my relationship with Daddy taken away.

The first wrong move I made in dealing with my latest predicament was to tell someone from my Navigator group. The second, and perhaps the most thoughtless mistake was that the person I told was a sixteen year-old girl I was discipling. Naturally, she felt inclined to help and told her parents. Nick, the leader of our Navigator group found out and chastised me for inappropriately burdening this young believer. But what was more troubling to him was the fact that I had been too afraid to tell my parents about my problem.

"Were you abused as a child?" he asked. The question caught me by surprise, as I did not understand its relevance to the issue.

Was I abused?

Rather than dwell on this complex question, I was more concerned about the trouble I would be in when Daddy found out. A few weeks earlier I had learned that Nick had met Daddy at a conference in South Korea two years earlier. At the time, it had sounded like a nice coincidence. But now, as the reality of this connection stared me in the face, I resented the fact that the Christian world now appeared to be one tiny crammed little planet where everyone knew each other. How could one hide in such small space? Deciding it was important to avoid trouble, abuse seemed to be the perfect excuse for my actions.

"Yes," I answered after a long pause. Daddy was informed, he paid the phone bill with no questions asked, and I was quickly placed in counseling.

"Tell me about your childhood?" The counselor, a middle-aged woman who spoke English with ease had asked me as I sipped on a freshly brewed cup of coffee. I still didn't know what abuse meant, but had agreed to go through counseling as a way to explain my behavior. I still had difficulty relating to Mommy, and even though Daddy had said nothing about the phone bill, two strikes against me were too many. I feared it was only a matter of time before they would say it was impossible for them to continue to provide for me. But more than my livelihood and education, what I feared most was losing my relationship with them. That would mean rejection, and that I had failed to earn either love or daughterhood. Was it possible that Mama had been the only human being who could ever love me unconditionally? What about God? Did he love me at all?

"My mother died when I was six and a half."

Responding to the counselor's question, I realized that the statement I had just made was what, in my mind, defined me as person. It was as though everything had stopped when Mama had died. Like a withered tree, I was an emotional stump, dead as a dried up plant in the desert, with nothing to thrive on. This realization sparked angry feelings toward God whom I blamed for my suffering. I couldn't touch Him, so, over the years I had lashed out at every one who tried to love me. My friend Sara had once said that I seemed to push people away. She was right, for I unconsciously sabotaged every relationship that offered me any real love. The façade was that I was afraid to get hurt. But inside, it was as if I was throwing these expressions of love back at God, because they weren't as good as having Mama. Nothing could replace her!

"How does the loss of your mom make you feel?" the counselor asked.

Her insightful question jolted me. Had she been reading my mind?

Of course I was angry. I was mad enough at that moment that I wanted to throw my coffee cup at her for being callous.

Shaking my head instead, I told her I needed to go home.

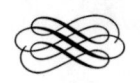

He Really Is My Father

The counseling sessions continued for several months. During the holidays, opportunities to spend time with Mommy presented themselves in unusual ways. The other children had moved out, and I no longer helped Daddy at the mission office. So when he was out, it was just Mommy and I. One afternoon, we walked to the city center in Utrecht because I needed some summer clothes.

"I don't think that is a good color on you," Mommy had said as I admired myself in a mirror. I had picked out yet another dark blue, low neck, close fitting business-like dress. This was how the popular girls in my high school had dressed. The one I had tried on before had been the same color and style, but with buttons all the way down the front. Mommy then handed me a flared, black floral dress.

"Try this. I know you like dark colors."

I went back to the dressing room and slipped on the delicate, hand-picked selection. It gave me an odd childlike sense that Mommy knew best. I looked in the mirror, admiring the elegant neckline that left just enough room for a short necklace. There was no cleavage, and even though the girls in college swore by the sexy, low necks, I didn't need to reveal that part of my body any more. Turning around, I watched the hem swirl. The dress was beautiful. When I walked out of the dressing room to show Mommy, it was almost like those long ago days when Mama used to help me get dressed in the morning.

We picked two more dresses before returning home. Thus began the many bonding experiences Mommy and I would share. Back in college, my grades continued to soar, as in my earlier years. Mommy and Daddy both celebrated my successes, adorning me with compliments and praise that increased my confidence in all I undertook. They encouraged me in every way, even allowing me to bring home new friends. This felt good. At the end of my third year in college, I needed to spend two semesters abroad as an exchange student and also do an internship. I chose to go to America.

Chapter 15

Prince Charming

Tucked away in eastern Ohio is the industrial city of Akron. Its main attraction to international students is its university, which is how I found myself there. As I prepared to leave for my exchange program, I discovered I needed to refer to Columbus and Cleveland as reference points, explaining to others in Holland that Akron wasn't too far from these larger, more cosmopolitan cities. I picked the University of Akron because, on the map, it appeared to be close to Philadelphia, Pennsylvania where two of my good friends from Kenya lived. Upon arrival, I was surprised to find that it would take more than a few hours to travel to Philadelphia by bus, and flying was beyond my means. With nothing else to do with my free time besides smell burning rubber from the tire factories, I browsed the Internet as a way to pass time. It was while doing this that I came across a Christian singles website.

While Mommy and Daddy remained a big part of my life, there was still a yearning in my heart for someone just for me. The Internet seemed to provide an ideal situation for me to list my best qualities and trust that whoever responded to my profile would likely know what he was getting into. Kurt was one of three men to show interest. I eliminated the other two because their values were different from mine. After several emails between Kurt and me, it was as though we had known each other forever. The only problem was that he lived in Alaska. We arranged to meet halfway and, after that, decide if we would move forward. I had one agenda on my mind when I arrived at Chicago's O'Hare airport. If we agreed that we still liked each other after meeting in person, marriage would have to be the next step.

I was shocked at first when I saw him standing at the end of the walkway past the Continental Airlines check-in desk. He seemed older and stockier than I had imagined. But determined to not let anything get in the way of my agenda, I quickly decided that looks weren't everything. I was not interested in a dating relationship, for I didn't even know what one looked like. I wanted a husband, and was convinced that this would be the answer to the ache in my heart. Here was a man who seemed to be head over heels in love with me. Kurt possessed all the qualities I had put together,

Prince Charming

much like a shopping list, for what I thought would be a perfect husband. He was a natural leader, just the trait any Christian woman would want in a man. And on top of that, he was romantic and intelligent.

Four months into our long distance relationship, I needed to decide what I was going to do for my internship. The exchange student semester was coming to an end. Akron Beacon Journal offered me a position in their Sales and Marketing department, but a car was required. I didn't even have a driver's license! With very little time left, I resorted to asking Kurt to see if there was anything I could do in Alaska. After all, we both wanted the relationship to continue, didn't we? He sent me a few companies' names and I contacted those companies. A few days later I received a phone call from the president of one of the companies asking if I was serious about moving to Alaska. It was the sign I had been waiting for.

When explaining to Daddy that Kurt was six years older than I and divorced, I quickly shifted to the fact that everything else had lined up so perfectly. Details like the door at Akron Beacon Journal closing, and the president of the company in Alaska swiftly responding to my resumé, were clear indications that God was leading me to be with this man. Offering me fatherly advice, Daddy told me not to rush into anything. So I gave the matter a couple days, and then bought my ticket to Anchorage, Alaska.

The snow on the ground had not completely melted, even though it was early May when I arrived. My first romantic weekend in the state was a camping trip near Girdwood, Alaska. We hiked through Crow Pass and pitched our tent near a glacier. Temperatures were still in the single digits up in the mountains, so our tents did not provide much comfort. I put on every piece of clothing I had brought and lay awake all night, expecting to die of hypothermia. Even Kurt, who had attended college in Fairbanks where it sometimes got to minus 50 degrees Fahrenheit, agreed that camping this time of the year was probably not a good idea. The following weekend we visited Soldotna, home of the world's largest salmon. There was not an end to what I could see in this vast state. The snow-covered mountains provided spectacular views everywhere you looked. Each morning, I was greeted by the sight of Mt. McKinley, the highest mountain in the U.S. It was certainly the most romantic state in all of America. With nature fostering every aspect of my new relationship, what could possibly go wrong?

Kurt's mother wasn't as enthralled as I was with this perfect match for her son. Her concern stemmed from the most misinformation I had ever encountered. In her own words, Africans danced around pots of boiling water with missionaries in them. This was not even racism, it was simply funny. And Kurt and I laughed it off, hoping that she would soon get over it. She did not. At one point, Kurt tried to illustrate just how ridiculous all this sounded. He had cut out and sent to her a picture of a woman wearing large rings around her neck with ears hanging down to her shoulders, a media image of a typical Maasai. In the note he had said it was a picture of me. Failing to see the humor, she had responded by telling him she was no longer his mother.

She was not the only one to disapprove of our biracial dating. A friend of his had claimed that the Bible forbade cross-cultural marriages, basing her argument on 2 Corinthians 6:14 ("Do not be yoked together with unbelievers. For what do righteousness and wickedness have in common? Or what fellowship can light have with darkness?"). Kurt's steadfast commitment in the midst of such opposition from those close to him only strengthened my conviction that he was the man for me. I knew for certain that it wouldn't be long before we were married. As weeks turned into months, however, I became restless. Why was it taking so long?

On Christmas day I called Daddy.

"How is Kurt doing?" he asked. I paused before answering. Kurt had been looking for a different job, which worried me because very likely he would have to move to a different state. He was in the court system, and there was not much room for advancement unless he moved. Most civil servants there just worked until they dropped dead, without getting ahead.

"What does he say about your relationship?" Daddy inquired, sounding concerned. That was the problem. Kurt had not been saying much about us. It had been almost a year since we had met, but he never discussed the future; or at least when he did, it never included me. Marriage was my only goal for this relationship, but Kurt was on a different schedule. Daddy suggested I go back to Holland for a while and allow Kurt time to think about his intentions, but the threat of being separated from him for any length of time made me uncomfortable. In desperation, I depended on daily communication with Kurt just to ensure he was thoroughly occupied with thoughts about me. Allowing him room to think about anything else was too risky. I had succeeded in getting him to love me, and I would do everything I could to make sure I didn't lose him.

Unfortunately, my internship was coming to an end, and I needed to go back to Groningen to graduate. My company offered me a permanent position if I was willing to come back to Alaska. This to me was further confirmation that God was in favor of my desire to be with Kurt. But as I prepared for my trip to Holland, a position in Todd County Court System in Minnesota opened up, and Kurt was invited for an interview.

Prince Charming

Restless in Groningen, I called Alaska every day anxious to know if there had been any news from Minnesota. The ten-hour time difference made it hard to connect with Kurt. Or was he avoiding me? I flew back to Alaska at the beginning of March to find that Kurt had been offered the position and would be moving to Minnesota at the end of that month. For days I couldn't eat, switching between fasting and simply not having an appetite. Over the weekend, I put on my brave face, not wanting him to see how desperate I felt. We cleaned his house and packed his belongings. He was completely excited about his new role, while I was terrified about what lay ahead—the inevitable separation when he went to Minnesota. I had barely survived the month in Holland. The disparity in our emotions was enormous.

Ten months after Kurt's departure, I left Alaska to start a new job in St. Paul, Minnesota. When my boss in Alaska had mentioned a few months earlier that our company was on the verge of cutting staff due to financial issues, it was just one more sign for me to pursue my stalling relationship. Surely if I could just remind him of how great things had been before I moved to Alaska, then perhaps he would want me again! Had I scared him off when I pushed him to make a decision? The relationship was going to be different this time. There would be no ultimatums, no phone calls each day. I was going to be the patient girl he wanted me to be.

Once in Minnesota I discovered that things were indeed different. None of Kurt's friends even knew I existed. If anything, they were surprised that I knew nothing about the other woman.

"911. Can you state your emergency?" The voice on the other end of the line was firm and urgent. I burst into painful sobs. A lump lodged in my throat, preventing me from responding.

"Ma'am, what is the problem?" the person continued.

"I'm so sorry," I said amidst sobs.

"Ma'am, calm down and tell me what's wrong!"

"I…I tried to kill myself."

"OK. Calm down. Can you tell me what you took?"

"Twenty-four Excedrin. My heart is racing. Can you help? Please…"

"Ma'am, it is OK. Try and calm down. What else did you take?"

"A glass of wine. Maybe two."

"Is anyone one else at home with you?"

"No."

"We are sending help right away. Keep talking to me. What else did you take?"

"Nothing else...but...I went to the garage and started my car..."

"Did you sit in the car?"

"No. I started the engine and then lay down on the floor."

I could hear sirens coming in the direction of my apartment. The man on the phone continued to ask questions. I was terrified. That morning I had driven back from Albany where Kurt lived, having confronted him about the other woman. He had offered no apology. It was not that I hadn't sensed the drift in our relationship. Months before he moved to Minnesota, I knew his heart had long grown cold.

God was really the issue. I believed He owed me for all the wrongs in my life. And now He had withheld the one thing that I desired most of all—someone for me. Maybe there were reasons why God had not chosen for Kurt to be my husband. But just for once couldn't I have something I wanted? I yearned for God to prove He cared about me. After all, was anything too hard for the Lord? Since nothing was, there could only be one explanation. God had chosen to let me down despite all the tears I had cried. Like an infant left alone in the crib, I felt forgotten. I had been screaming and yelling out to God who, in my opinion, had simply turned His back on me where it mattered most. And because of that, I had tried to get back at God by using the only method I could think of. By taking my own life, I would finally get His attention.

The loud knock on my door came as a relief. As three paramedics walked in carrying a stretcher, my knees gave in, causing me to tumble to the floor. When I woke up later that afternoon, a nurse was standing by my bed monitoring an intravenous tube above my head. She explained that there had been enough Excedrin in my blood to kill me. Had I really wanted to die? The thought frightened me. A few weeks later, I ended up at a Bible camp where a friend had invited me to attend a conference. The camp director, sensing my need to find new direction in my life, offered me a job while I considered my next step. Built on the shore of Lake Carlos in Alexandria, Minnesota, Mount Carmel Bible Camp provided unlimited access to the outdoors, which I enjoyed, and a serenity that can only be found alongside clear, cool waters. The personnel at the camp were hospitable and gentle, not demanding an explanation for the tears that showed up on my face at the most inappropriate moments. This freedom to grieve allowed me time and space to heal my wounded heart. It was at this camp that I found courage to start over.

Chapter 16

HE REALLY IS MY FATHER

From left: Wim, Susie and Margreet

Daddy had cried with joy when I described my experience at the Bible camp. He and Mommy later came to visit me there. As I talked about my plans for the future, Daddy had encouraged my goal to further my education. While looking into the possibility of beginning a graduate program, I found out about a job opening at Bethel University. As an employee I would be eligible for a tuition benefit. This opportunity made it possible for me to earn my master's degree without needing a student loan. Daddy accompanied me to my new students' orientation, and then, on their way back to Holland, they had waited for me in the car as I interviewed for my job at Bethel before I dropped them off at the airport.

As challenges in my new life took me to untrodden paths, it was time to rekindle my relationship with God. I went back to what I had learned through the Navigators, reading my Bible regularly and meeting with younger believers to pass on what had been handed down to me. It was at this point in my life that I met Pete. I needed help, especially with the boys in the Bible study group I had started at my house. Pete had some experience with Navigators, so I knew we would have the same vision. But then one day, out of the blue, he told me God had showed him that a white American woman would be a better wife for him if he ever went to serve overseas as a missionary. I knew he had a heart for missions and a desire to marry someday. While I would have welcomed the possibility of being Pete's wife, it shocked me to hear that God had eliminated me on the basis of my color and nationality. So once again, I sought out a counselor.

"Does God show favoritism?"

As I sat in Ann's office, this was the question that had been plaguing me. She handed me some tissue to wipe my sore eyes. I had struggled with my relationship with God over the years, wondering if He cared about me. My doubt about God's love had only, up until now, revolved around His inability to meet my need to belong. I believed He had purposely taken everything away, just like Mother and Father had always done. Daddy had been able to provide a partial sense of belonging, whenever I was with him or heard his reassuring voice over the phone. But like the dry, parched soil in the semi-desert region of Turkana, thriving on the occasional rainfall as it soaked through the cracks left by years of drought, my euphoria would quickly give way to endless thirst. Was I so emotionally malnourished that, like the poster child of the media coverage for Africa, I was easily diseased by every emotional disaster that came my way? Maybe; but that was irrelevant to me now.

All I could think of as I sat in Ann's office was that God saw my skin color and called it bad. Never before had I considered the fact that He might steer others away from me because He had made me second class. If Pete was right, then I had no dignity left. When Ann asked why this hurt so much, I explained that I could handle being rejected by people, but if God was rejecting me, where else could I go?

"What if Pete is wrong?" Ann asked gently.

Absorbed in my own feelings of inadequacy, I elevated everyone else, accepting everything they said about me or did to me. In my mind, I was all wrong. How had I come to value myself so little? The continuous tape in my head was no longer necessary. I was living up to those words so engraved into my soul; *I am unworthy.* But how did God fit into all this?

That night, I tossed restlessly for hours, unable to fall asleep. At around midnight, I picked up the phone and called Daddy like I always did when in distress. It was morning for him, so I knew I'd catch him before he left for the day. I admired his unwavering faith in God, but struggled to apply such trust in my own spiritual life. When I replaced the receiver, I picked up my Bible and opened the book of Matthew to chapter seven as Daddy had suggested. Verses 9-11 said, "Which of you, if his son asks for bread, will give him a stone? Or if he asks for a fish, will give him a snake? If you, then, though you are evil, know how to give good gifts to your children, how much more will your Father in heaven give good gifts to those who ask him!"

He Really Is My Father

I closed my eyes, still feeling angry with God as I had for a long time. I recalled my conversation with Ann. What if Pete was wrong? *Well, if God had no part in steering Pete away from me, there was still the issue with Kurt.* God had not given me the husband I had been asking for. If He was my Father, why wasn't He behaving the way Matthew 7:9-11 was saying He should?

Reflecting back on my conversation with Daddy, it occurred to me that I really trusted him. Our relationship had grown over the years through spending time together and communicating on a consistent basis. It was funny to think that I depended so much on the constant assurance through Daddy's letters and words that he loved me. I needed to hear it often. I laughed as the similarities between how I viewed God and how I had viewed Daddy became clear to me. I had learned some valuable principles through the Navigators, such as reading the Bible consistently and memorizing Scripture. Those were good practices, but for me, becoming God's child was much more than spiritual disciplines. It was a bit like becoming adopted into a family when you are older, just as in my case with the Bouw family. Children raised by biological parents have a natural relationship and know how to relate to their parents. Adopted children, especially if they are older, bring past experiences into the relationship. When I went to live with Mommy and Daddy, I had expected to be treated in the same way Mother and Father had treated me. I was so afraid to make mistakes, fearing I would be punished or sent away. My expectations of them were based on my previous experience. I had not been a clean slate, the way an adopted infant would be.

I looked at the clock on my night stand. It was two in the morning. Frustrated with my insomnia, I decided there was no use staying in bed. I picked up a book I had been trying to read, "The Path of Loneliness" by Elizabeth Elliot, and went upstairs and settled in my favorite chair across from the television. I placed the remote control close by, just in case I decided to watch something instead. Elizabeth Elliot talked about contentment as a single woman in a way that stirred up resentfulness in me. She was married to her third husband, and I had not even been granted one. I could see why she would be at peace with God. As for me, there was still the issue with Kurt. This reminded me of another incident that had sent me running to Ann's office.

"What is bothering you this time?" Ann had asked sitting in her usual chair close to the pastor's desk in the church office where we usually met. I had received news that a close friend had just become engaged. She was six years younger than I and, even though I had been happy for her, I felt forgotten by God. Why wouldn't He grant me the desire of my heart? I had prayed for years that this need would be fulfilled, convinced that it would be the one thing that would complete me.

"You know what I think, Susie?" Ann had begun with the authority of an experienced counselor. "I think even if God gave you a husband today, you would still find other reasons to be mad at Him. You don't really trust Him. The reason you don't trust Him is because you don't know Him."

Do I really know God?

With Elizabeth Elliot's book still in my hand, I pondered this thought. I was amazed at how much sense Ann's words seemed to make now. I had been relating to God in exactly the same way I had related to Mother and Father. They had withheld things from me and never seemed to want me to enjoy anything. I had brought these experiences and expectations into my relationship with God. And just as I had needed to learn to relate to Mommy and Daddy, I would need to learn to relate to God. Getting to know Him was not only about reading His word, but experiencing a relationship with Him.

Daddy had written me letters over the years, but I had to learn how he reacted to my mistakes, something I had feared. I didn't really know him until I experienced how he behaved in different situations. This meant, first of all, that it was natural for me to react the way I did toward God. It would take time before I could really say I knew His heart. I needed to experience Him in different situations in my life. Then, with time, I would need to get rid of the habits I had brought from my previous relationships, and replace them with habits that reflected my knowledge and understanding of who He was as the father described in Matthew 7:9-11.

The memory of the time when Daddy had told me I wouldn't be going back to Leicester flashed through my mind. It seemed ridiculous now to think of how upset I had been. I had expected the worst, filtering everything through my experience with Mother and Father. Was it possible that if I could hear God's assurance of His own love for me over and over, I might come to trust Him even more than I did Daddy? Would experiencing Him over time bring me to that place where I longed to be? The answer suddenly became obvious. It would be a long process of walking side by side with God, much like in my relationship with Daddy, before I could finally say that God really is my Father. And that is how my true journey of daughterhood began.

That summer, I wrote Daddy a long letter, thanking him for the role he had played in helping me find my true Father. In November of that year, I met Steve. We emailed each other for a month after my friend Nancy connected us with each other. When Steve laid his eyes on me for the first time outside Bruegger's Bagels in Roseville, Minnesota, it was obvious that he fell in love with me at first sight. So, it wasn't a surprise when we became engaged six months later and then married on September 29, 2001. Mommy and Daddy walked me down the aisle at the same Bible Camp where I had found a new beginning. Eighteen months after our honeymoon, Steve woke up to an urgent call from me.

"Honey, would you come down for a second?"

"What's wrong?" he had responded sleepily. It was 6:00 in the morning on a Saturday, and I had gone downstairs to read so as not to disturb him as I tossed from side to side in discomfort. Sharp pains in my groin had been waking me up every morning for about a month. The doctor had labeled my discomfort as Braxton Hicks, describing it as a false labor common in the third trimester of most pregnancies. But on this morning, I knew it had to be more than just practice labor.

"I think it is time to call the hospital!"

"What?"

Steve ran down, bringing me the phone. I called the nurse line and began timing my contractions, which became aggressive within half an hour. My tolerance for any pain is minimal, so by 9:00 a.m. I convinced the nurse I would be better off at the hospital.

Seraiah was born at 5:05 p.m. that Saturday, March 22, 2003. As we beheld his little face in awe, I remembered how excited we had been to finally learn that I had conceived. During the nine months of trying to have a baby, it had finally dawned on me that pregnancy didn't just happen when two people got together. God had to have been involved. It was this realization that solidified for me the truth of Jeremiah 1:5, "Before I formed you in the womb I knew you…" My own birth may have been a result of rape, but God allowed the conception to happen, and therefore, He knew me and wanted me to be born.

Two days later we brought Seraiah home. Our first phone call as parents came later that evening.

"Hello!" I said as soon as I picked up the phone.

"Praise the Lord!" It was Daddy using his favorite phrase, even at such a late hour as 1:00 a.m. Holland time.

Five-and-a-half months later, when the phone rang and I heard it was my brother Gisbert, I knew immediately that something was wrong. My fears were confirmed, as I learned that Daddy had died after twelve days in the hospital following a stroke. The last time I had talked to him had been July 11 that same year, when I called thinking it was Gisbert's birthday. He had laughed, reminding me that dates in Holland were written differently, which meant that 7/11 was actually the seventh of November. I was just beginning to really be part of the whole family by remembering birthdays and other important events.

He Really Is My Father

When I arrived at Schipol International Airport to attend Daddy's funeral, it was such an odd feeling to be picked up by someone I hardly knew. For fifteen years, Daddy had always been there for me. While he had never tucked me in bed at night as a child, or helped me remove my first tooth, he had been present for all my significant milestones and events as an adult: coming to visit me after my breakup with Kurt, taking me to my orientation for graduate school, attending my master's degree commencement, giving me away on my wedding day, calling to congratulate me when my son was born…he had been my Daddy!

As we drove in silence toward Utrecht, the overcast clouds and the pouring rain reflected our dejected mood. Mommy met us at the door, carrying herself gracefully in her typical pastor's wife's role. *Did it have to be this way?* Everything was so surreal. Daddy's shoes remained underneath the kitchen island, just as though he was about to wear them like he had always done. I went upstairs to Mommy's room to change into a black dress. Daddy's shaver and toothbrush remained at the sink, undisturbed. Even the room smelled as though he was just walking through the door. His absence could be felt throughout the house, and it felt wrong, because there was so much evidence of his life.

The hearse arrived on schedule, and we followed it in a convoy. Children played out in the rain at a nearby school. Their joyous laughter served as a rude reminder that, for some, it was a normal day. The 750 people who showed up for the funeral service were a comforting reminder of how Daddy had touched the lives of so many. Later, when nine of us (Mommy, children, and spouses) held hands and took turns praying around Daddy's grave before his coffin was lowered down, I felt more connected to this family than I ever had in all of Daddy's life. Here I was at the gravesite, participating in the most private ceremony a family can endure, while the extended family waited at the visitor center. This experience gave me a true sense of belonging. When it was my turn to pray, all I could think of was what a privilege it was to be counted as one of the Bouw's children. *He really had been my father.*

About the Author

Susie Brooks was born in Kenya. Having received her education in the Netherlands and the USA, she teaches at Bethel University in St. Paul, Minnesota, and speaks on topics relating to Women in Kenya, the Sanctity of Life, and God's Fatherhood. In addition to books, she is also a screenplay writer. Susie has lived in Kenya, England, the Netherlands, and now the USA with her husband and son. http://www.aseka.com

To order additional copies of this title call:
1-877-421-READ (7323)
or please visit our web site at
www.pleasantwordbooks.com

Printed in the United States
83010LV00001B/37-60/A